PRAISE FOR MARTHA & CHRIS
FROM REAL CUSTOMERS AND AFFILIATES

"Martha and Chris have wisdom—and it shows through. Their dedication to the achievement of their own customers is obvious as is their desire for your success."

—JAY CONRAD LEVINSON, Father of Guerrilla Marketing, Entrepreneur

"Martha is a force. She's using her passion and formula to have a billion-dollar impact on small businesses. Grit, a framework and the power of mentoring, is realized in this book."

—PROMISE PHELON, Chairperson, Sueno Growth Partners

"Chris has worked with me to refine my sales approach to improve my results using Customertopia principles…and I consider myself to be an excellent sales person! Now I'm an even better one, more focused and assured of what my prospects and customers want to know to solve their image and presence challenges."

—MARCELLA SCHERER, Image and Presence Speaker, Coach and Consultant

"We were reaching out to the same referral sources and getting the same results. Having worked with Chris and Martha for a year now and we now have a new billing model, a growth strategy with measurable goals, and a renewed vision of what success looks like. Our referral base has grown, and referrals are up significantly. We are at the point of looking to add another care manager to help. I would recommend Chris and Martha to anyone wanting to grow—but really for anyone wanting to see their business from a higher vantage point."

—BYRON CORDES, Sage Care Management

"We began our relationship as vendors, and as we worked together, it transcended into aligned partnership. Martha and Chris have the same vision for their business as I do—we believe our businesses become successful only when our customers succeed. When your customer is front and center in your business... in everything you do...your business transforms."

—KARLA MERRELL, The Event Maximizer, CEO, Meet and Greet Events LLC

"I've worked with Martha and Chris in the past to advance my businesses, and I'm stepping in to do more together. Their focus on my customer, team and myself means developing and advancing my three businesses becomes easier, more fruitful and fun, too."

—ANNE SANSEVERO, President, HealthSense LLC

"I've had the privilege of working alongside many great marketing minds. Martha and Chris stand out with their unique talent to make understanding your customer the centerpiece of your business and then building everything you do from that perspective."

—JILL LUBLIN, 4 times Best-Selling Author, International Speaker, Master Publicity Strategist

"Working with Martha and Chris I've stepped up our marketing, sales, team development and customer-focused results. The business has experienced a revenue increase of over six figures and operates smoothly when I'm traveling as my team understands their roles in delivering an exceptional customer experience."

—WELDON WULSTEIN, CPA, Wulstein Financial Services and Co.

"We've worked with Martha and Chris to accelerate our business results through coaching and positioning our construction business. Then we took what we've created together and integrated it into our brochure and website. They are easy to work with, flexible and patient. They were with us every step of the way through our busy business, and I truly appreciate that."

—DAWN REED, Flegel's Construction

"Walking into your women's leadership retreat, Lead Her Up, I was nervous and didn't know what to expect. At the end of the event, I felt more confident in myself as a leader and got clarity on what my next steps should be! It was refreshing to be around women who genuinely care and support one another. In those three days, I stepped foot on the beach for the first time, made lifelong connections and learned a great deal about myself and my business. Thank you. Thank you. Thank you. And so it is."

—ALLYESE GOODWIN, Marie Creative

"Chris and Martha of Wide Awake Business attract powerful and accomplished people to their work, which is why I choose theirs over other programs, a winning (and rare) combination of business smarts, integrity, heart, humor and spirit. The quality of their clientele is a perfect mirror of the quality of their coaching and events."

—LICIA BERRY, CEO, Daughters of Earth Women's Leadership Institute

"As an affiliate partner of Wide Awake Business—Martha and Chris—we work together to put new prospects into the hands of Wide Awake Business' customers. We make sure everything we do on-line to attract new prospects speaks the language of the customer. In a noisy, crazy on-line world, putting the customer in the center of your conversation ensures results."

—JASON HALL, Five Channels

"Martha and Chris figured out my Super Power. My expertise is Medicare. Not sexy or exciting and often considered boring. I needed to stand out by showing my friendly, quirky, unique service-first style. After personally struggling, Martha creatively delivered the top concerns that worry Medicare clients. Together they defined my business and created an identity geared to attract my top 5 prospects. Standing out is my new normal. On top of everything is my new website, I have a clear direction. They knocked it out of the ballpark!"

—TRACY BLACKBURN, AskTracyB

CUSTOMERTOPIA

How to Create an Easier, Simpler,
More **PROFITABLE** Business

MARTHA HANLON & CHRIS WILLIAMS

Published by
The Pensiero Press

All rights reserved. No part of this publication may be reproduced,
stored in a retrieval system, or transmitted in any form or by
any means, electronic, mechanical, photocopying, recording or
otherwise without the written permission of the publisher.

https://www.Facebook.com/WideAwakeBusiness/
https://twitter.com/WideAwakeBiz
https://in.linkedin.com/company/Wide-Awake-Business
https://www.linkedin.com/in/MarthaHanlon/
https://www.linkedin.com/in/ChrisWilliams10/

ISBN: 978-1-7329382-3-6

This book is designed to provide information about the subject matter covered.
It is sold with the understanding the authors and publisher are not engaged
in rendering legal, accounting, financial or other professional services. If legal
or other expert assistance is required, the services of a competent professional
should be sought.

You are everything.

CONTENTS

———————————————PART FOUR: BUILD YOUR CUSTOMER MACHINE

WHAT EXACTLY IS CUSTOMERTOPIA?

Come with us for a moment. You'll love where we're about to take you.

Imagine this. Your business bursts with all the customers you want. They come more easily than in the past. You love working with them, and they love working with you. They pay…and on time! Your business isn't overwhelming you or stressing you out. At least not most of the time. You have a plan for the business. It's set up and running like a disciplined, slick engine of commerce. You have team tending to the details. You're leading them, delivering your highest value to your business. You find yourself doing less of the *do* and more of the things really making a difference. You choose which clients you want to work with. You're hitting your goals. You have time…make time…for family and friends. You take vacations, go to plays and have some time to exercise. You even have a little time just for yourself. You feel and are successful on your terms. Life feels pretty darn good.

You've just experienced Customertopia.

Customertopia creates those nearly perfect qualities we all want in our business, ones designed to reduce the problems most small business owners live with. It's not a perfectly perfect place. Yet, as you build towards Customertopia, you'll experience the improvements you've sought for yourself.

Customertopia means you have a realistic blueprint for successfully running your business. A business that's easier, simpler and more profitable.

Which brings us to you.

How is your business doing?

Do you have all the customers you want? Are prospects easy to find and

1

engage? Are you busy, not feeling overwhelmed, overrun or stressed out? Or is your business running you…instead of you running your business?

Perhaps you're successful, hitting all your goals. Maybe those goals are still in front of you.

CUSTOMERTOPIA CREATES THE EASIER, SIMPLER, MORE PROFITABLE BUSINESS YOU WANT.

If your business feels like it's taking a personal toll on you, trade it for Customertopia. If it feels like all you do is work, work, work on your business without the results and income you want, if you're sacrificing other aspects of your life, enter Customertopia. If you feel stuck, you've tried everything you know, understanding and implementing the very straight-forward steps of Customertopia will "unstick" you.

This book lays out how to build the business you want, hit your goals and do so without the overwhelming personal sacrifice you're currently making.

The key to Customertopia might not surprise you. You have probably heard it before, yet you might not be following what you've heard. The key to having a business working in Customertopia means…

…you've built *everything* about your business from the point-of-view of your customer.

Not some things. *Everything.*

You see, most small business owners have heard or read about making sure their business is a customer-centered business. These words you've heard. Yet, you haven't constructed your business that way or simply don't know how to do it. Building your business **from your customer in to you**, rather than from you out to your customer, means everything you build, and deliver is founded on your customer, who they are, what motivates them, their aspiration in the areas you serve and the problem they are trying to conquer.

IT'S TIME YOUR BUSINESS STOPPED RUNNING YOU!

Could this be what your world looks like and why your business isn't totally, 100% customer-centered? Let's see if the description below fits you a bit.

At some point, you decided to go into business for yourself. You have a skill, a product and a service you are great at creating and delivering. You are an amazing coach, care manager, chiropractor, financial advisor, marketing expert, sales consultant, real estate agent, property manager, content creator, copywriter, court reporter, weight-loss expert, back-office systems developer, networking designer...whatever you do. You are quite convinced "anybody" or "everybody" needs what you had to offer. Because you're very good at it. You went looking for people to buy your product or service because those people really, really needed it, you firmly believed.

You told them all about your product or service. You shared the details about what you do. Maybe you were a little nervous as you approached the part about what you service costs, but you spoke. Words came out.

YOUR CUSTOMERS' WANTS MUST BE THE FOCUS OF YOUR BUSINESS.

You called them once, maybe *only* once because you didn't want to "bother" them, to be a pest. If they were interested in working with you, they would certainly call you back.

Yet, they didn't. Fewer prospects turned into customers than you envisioned, and you're not sure why.

The answer to why this happened is simple, and the change in your business to create the results you want is pretty simple, too.

Your prospects failed to engage with you because you were busy telling them things that weren't important to them. You were telling them about you, and they don't care about you...yet. You shared all the details about your service, and they don't care about your service...yet. You asked them to buy, and they weren't ready yet. You moved a little too fast. You honestly believed them when they said, "I'll call you when I'm ready." Yet, they didn't call, and they won't call simply because they became overwhelmed by other responsibilities, other problems (not because they were trying to avoid you).

The statement most important to your prospect was skimmed over or not touched at all. The most important thing to your prospect...what they care about more than anything is...

...themselves.

They want their problem, challenge, issue, obstacle (whatever they call it) removed. They want to know the **outcome** of working with you, how their lives change when they spend money with you. They want to know their problem goes away, and frankly, the vast majority of your prospects don't care how you do it, just as long as you do it.

Customertopia means just about everything you say and do regarding your company is created from your customer's perspective. Everything.

FORSAKE YOUR POINT-OF-VIEW IN FAVOR OF YOUR IDEAL CUSTOMER'S POINT-OF-VIEW.

How you introduce yourself at a networking event. What you write and where you place your copy on your website. How your service is created. What you say when you call or email your prospect. How you craft your "Elevator Speech." What you say in your biography.

The key to creating all of this means you must have…

…insights into the mind of your customer.

Building a customer-centered business, creating your Customertopia, implies you know precisely who your customer is (and that description doesn't start with "anyone" or "everyone"). You understand how they behave in your area of expertise, not how they behave with you (we'll get to that later, just not right now). You recognize what motivates them, what they aspire to achieve in your area of excellence (not just the surface aspirations, the deep and true emotional ones). You understand the problem they have, the one they want to solve (which, because you're the expert, you might know isn't their problem at all, but you can't solve a problem they don't recognize they have).

You'll know them better than you know your kids!

You'll *think like your customer*. You'll *act like your customer*. And you'll *build your business for your customer*.

Which just so happens to be how this book is structured. Amazing, right?

DEMYSTIFY YOUR BUSINESS

You are about to demystify and significantly reduce the difficult, complex and less profitable ways you've been conducting your business. Through this book, we're going to break down all the steps into specific actions for you. Now you'll have the answers to turn things around in your business, to experience the ultimate—an easier, simpler, more profitable business.

Like anything new you embark on, Customertopia might cause you to feel something's missing. You're not "getting" something. We promise you we'll be clear and precise as we walk you through your roadmap to a more fulfilling business. We're going to show you your business constructed from a different perspective, that of your customer's. So, of course, you might question if Customertopia works.

We want you to know we've worked with 5,324 small business owners just like you (yes, we count...you should, too) and have created $628,000,000 in business for them as we write this. We've developed this approach over 14 years. We use this system ourselves and use it with all our clients.

We want to transform the way you think and act about your business. More importantly, we want to transform the way you attract new customers. Where would your business be—where would any business be—without customers?

The secret to a thriving business lies in attracting customers. The secret to attracting customers is to have insights into their minds.

Let's go get you some customers. All you want. All you deserve.

IT'S ALL ABOUT YOUR CUSTOMER

You're holding the blueprint for success in your hands right now.

Customertopia shows you the steps to take to get more customers, and do it more easily, simply and more profitably. Unlike many complicated systems out there, Customertopia grows by implementing four constructs:

- Gain the Customertopia Mindset

- Think Like Your Customer

- Act Like Your Customer

- Build For Your Customer

First, as with so many transformations in business and life, we begin with you and your mindset, **Gain The Customertopia Mindset**. As Carol Dweck, Ph.D. said in her book, *Mindset,* "...it's not just our abilities and talent that bring us success." The power of your beliefs propels your choices and directions. Yes, we'll likely be adjusting some of your beliefs as we work together, ones you recognize and others you don't. Now we're not psychologists and won't attempt to be ones so no worries about that. Adopting Customertopia will require you to abandon some ways of thinking and adopt better ones. Be open to transformation.

THE ULTIMATE BUSINESS MEANS THINGS ARE EASIER, SIMPLER AND MORE PROFITABLE FOR YOU.

Foremost, you'll discover how to **Think Like Your Customer**. You will seek insights into the mind of your customer. Nothing else will be more important in this book and in your business than this step. Get this right, and you'll immediately notice a difference in your business. Think Like Your Customer becomes your foundation for everything wonderful, everything easier, simpler and more profitable. Without this as your solid foundation you'll wander away from your customer. You'll experience difficulty finding prospects, connecting on a true level and engaging in a meaningful way. It's a lot like building a house. Build a strong foundation so you won't be banging away on something that will eventually fall apart.

With your foundation in place, you're ready to **Act Like Your Customer**. You'll put your customer insights into action, use them in your business, in your marketing and in your sales. These actions target dramatically increasing the number of customers you attract to your business—and that means more revenue, which translates into a very happy you.

Finally, **Build For Your Customer** hands you Customer Machines aligned to different occupations. They'll guide you to restructure your business to make it more machine-like, and less "something new every day." Imagine if a McDonald's owner had to figure out how she wanted to make burgers each day she walked into her restaurant. McDonald's has a process, and this section will show you how to construct one for yourself, too.

With these four steps in place, never again will you sense you're owned by your business, feel completely overwhelmed and without an idea how to make things just a little easier. Instead, you'll focus on how to serve your customers even more fabulously.

As you work through the book, you'll discover a few new tools to make your learning easier and maybe more fun.

A TYPICAL BUSINESS DAY IN THE LIFE
OF A CUSTOMERTOPIA BUSINESS PERSON

Visualize you're having the perfect day. A super-wonderful day you want to live again and again. You are standing in front of an audience of Ideal Prospects. Their heads are up, attentive. They are taking mad notes, asking questions and nodding in agreement. You make them an offer that will eliminate their most vexing problem, the one you've been discussing for an hour. Before you can even finish your sentence, people are rushing to the back of the room to grab the offer. When you finish, the room buzzes with excitement, and you receive a thunderous clap of applause. More than 50% of the room grabs your offer as they fully realize it...and you...are the solution to the problem they've been living with for too long. You leave with orders totally $24,876!

Maybe speaking isn't your "thing," and you'd prefer to reach your Ideal Prospects in other ways. Then try on this perfect day. You make a list of all the people and businesses capable of referring business to you. The list surprises you in its length. You begin to reach out to those on the list. You call to set appointments, saying just the right things. They agree to take an appointment with you to speak in greater detail. They are intrigued as you solve a problem for their customer, one they are not qualified to solve themselves. They agree to try you and send you a few prospects to test this new relationship and your results. Of course, you nail it. You begin to receive more and more referrals from these sources. Soon over 85% of your business comes through this active referral system you've created. Your business doubles and then triples.

As you head back to your office with your leads from the speaking event and the referrals from your referral partners, you call your dedicated, efficient virtual assistant who tells you he's received four calls from people who would like to interview you for their podcast. "Book it," you say! Then he shares that your book marketing company called too, and they've lined up an amazing book signing tour for you, supporting it with a stunning social media strategy. He calls your book publisher and tells them to print another 1,000 books.

With all these new customers coming in the door, you begin to reach out to your team to assign the work. Mary, Ed, Susan and Jennifer agree to the deliverables and timeframe. Brittany will project management all the deliverables to insure everything happens on time and on budget. Your accountant confirms the value of the orders you've brought back and approves the costs to deliver the projects.

Later that same day, you call your Mentor as today is your scheduled appointment. You report all your slam-dunk results, and she moves the discussion towards how you can become an even more skilled, polished leader. You love her ideas and know just how to implement them, what to adjust in your behavior and actions.

Before you end your day, you call home. Your spouse suggests you revel in your thrilling day by heading out for a celebration dinner...or would you prefer a weekend get-away? "Why not do both?" you say. So you head out that very weekend, returning on Tuesday. When you walk in your office and check in with your team, everything has been running smoothly without you as your team knows exactly what they should be doing and are doing it.

How did that little ride feel? Pretty great, I imagine. Plus, I'm betting it's miles from how you're working now. A little dream? Yes, and a really good dream. Everything you've just imagined becomes possible when you begin to think, act and build like and for your customer. Yes, work is required. But it's the right work, not mounds of new things to do. You'll actually discover that when you build your business from Customertopia, you'll be doing fewer things. They'll be the right few things.

OUR PROMISE TO YOU

We grew our own business chops as a marketing executive (Martha) and small business owner and sales expert (Chris). We both left Corporate America as our hearts were drawn to small business owners. We've worked for ourselves since 2002, and with each other since 2008. We both feel very lucky to have had the privilege of working with over 5,324 small business owners as of this writing. And while that's pretty special, our coach asked us "what did you do for them?" Such a better question! So to this day we track it. What we've done for those 4,891 clients is enable them to generate an additional $638 million dollars by acquiring new customers and strengthening the bond with existing customers. Our clients are out there making the world a better place.

Sure, we've had our ups-and-downs. Each makes us smarter, able to adjust as the world changes. The more you know, the more you're equipped to compete and make the world a better place your way. Therefore, we want you to be armed with the best wisdom a small business owner can have, generated through practical information, vibrating insights, commanding ideas and mind-blowing questions. We'll be your personal coach, walking you step-by-step through the *Customertopia* formula. And we won't be far away when you want support after you've read this book (see Part Five of this book...we're not far away).

We're betting most self-help and business book buyers grab a book expecting it will change their lives. Then they only read a few pages, believe they have the full idea and put the book on the nightstand where it enjoys the company of seven other half-read books.

• • • • • • • • • • • • • • • • • **SALES SIDEBAR**

Throughout the book, we'll be driving you to our website (WideAwake Business.com/Resources) and a resources page to see lots of cool tools. We're sending you there for a good reason. We want you to be familiar with us by, first, using our website so when you're ready to advance to the next steps, and want some help, you'll be familiar with and connected to us. What are you doing in your business to drive people to your website? Just role modeling for you!

We decided to offer you TABLE 1 as a way of keeping Customertopia from becoming one of your half-read books. If you read this Table, your odds of reading the entire book go up 533% (okay, we made that up). Your odds go up because you'll know what you'll miss by not reading beyond this page.

TABLE 1: BOOK OVERVIEW

	What You'll Find	Who It's Best Suited For
Part One: Gain the Customertopia Mindset	All true, permanent transformations begin with your mind. This book asks you to transform how you do business. Your mind is the first place the transformation must begin.	The reader whose brain says evil, untrue things like "you can't do that," or "you're not good enough," or "this will never work for you." In other words…most of us!
Part Two: Think Like Your Customer	Your customer doesn't think like you. Part Two shares how they think, what they want from you and how you can discover what's really driving them.	Business owners who struggle to connect with more prospects, fail to garner attention when they speak, convert a website visitor to a caller or connect on social media platforms.
Part Three: Act Like Your Customer	Once you know how your customers think you must transform every nook and cranny of your business to act like your customers' act…how they buy, rather than how you sell.	You…if you think, act and conduct your business from your point-of-view.
Part Four: Build For Your Customer	You're ready to transform how you've built your business because a business built to engage your Ideal Customer…built to their needs rather than just yours… creates a stronger alignment and more sales from your Ideal Customer.	Small business owners without any system or a system built to make business easier for you rather than make it easier for your customers to engage and buy from you.
Part Five: An Easier, Simpler, More Profitable Business for You & Your Business	Here's the pay-off for your hard work to create a fully customer-centered business… your final steps to transform your business into a Customertopia of profitability.	Business owners who want to trade their complicated, often overwhelming, less profitable business for one that's easier, simpler and more profitable… and with fewer roads leading to you.

HOW TO SPEND YOUR TIME, ENERGY AND MONEY

Throughout this book, you'll find tons of directions on things you will be doing—from listening to your customers, to developing your Elevator Speech (hook), to moving from a sales model to a buying model, to constructing a machine instead of a random way of operating, and much more. Holy Smokes, you say!! That could be overwhelming. Please stop and look carefully at TABLE 2. No matter where you are in your business, no matter how long you've been in business, you'll gain clarity around where you should best spend your time and resources by following this chart. This will take the pressure off. You don't have to do everything now!

TABLE 2: FOCUS AREAS		
Experience	**Years in Business/ Revenue**	**Area of Focus**
Straddlers	Not in your business full-time; still in a j-o-b; revenue under $50K	**Part One: Gain The Customertopia Mindset** Focus on getting your mind on board believing you have the talent and desire to create a more carefully created business, built from your customers' perspective…so Customertopia is much more likely to happen and stick!
		Part Two: Think Like Your Customer Start right, right from the beginning by creating your business from your customers' perspective; their buying motivators are already built in; this is where you discover the steps to find out what your customer's are.
		Part Three: Act Like Your Customer You now know how your customers think…what they want; Part Three shows you step-by-step how to act like your customer and convert your selling process to a buying process (they aren't the same, you know). You must act like your customer to create that perfect alignment.

		TABLE 2: FOCUS AREAS
		Part Five: An Easier, Simpler, More Profitable Business If you're feeling overwhelmed, be assured you don't have to figure all of this out…not to mention do it…by yourself. Here's where you can find the assistance you want to grow the business you want.
Solopreneur	One-person business (You); fully dedicated to your business and engaged; making under $150K	**Part One: Gain The Customertopia Mindset** You've had some success yet struggle with how you can continue to grow because your mind keeps telling you things that hold you back.
		Part Two: Think Like Your Customer Cleaning up the most common error business owners make—communicating from your point-of-view—will show you your growth opportunity, and it doesn't require more spending or team.
		Part Three: Act Like Your Customer Once you know how to think as your customer thinks, you must act as they prefer for you to act (which is more like they act). Until you make this adjustment, your business will feel like a car out of alignment…you'll be pulling one way while the customers you want will be pulling another.
		Part Four: Build For Your Customer You might be working hard to build your business. We believe you're ready to step up to building your business correctly, right now, before it's bigger and more complex to adjust. Now' the right time to build your business for your customer.
		Part Five: An Easier, Simpler, More Profitable Business Yes, you want more customers. For sure. What you really, really want is a business that's easier, simpler and more profitable. That's the focus for you in Part Five.

TABLE 2: FOCUS AREAS		
Seasoned Solopreneur	One-person business (you); making between $150K and $300K	**Part One: Gain The Customertopia Mindset** Yep, you're doing pretty well for yourself, and you want to do even better. How often does your mindset hold you back? Right. Start your focus on business acceleration with an asset too many business owners overlook…how your mind manipulates you.
		Part Two: Think Like Your Customer You've accomplished so much as a solopreneur. To continue to grow through your efforts alone…without team…means it's time to work smarter. Getting the junk out of your business and replacing it with what's important to your customer leverages you in far more profitable ways.
		Part Three: Act Like Your Customer Thinking like your customer is great. Thinking then demands acting. Your customers understand themselves far more than they are willing to understand you. Speak and act like they want you to do. Part Three shows you the steps.
		Part Four: Build For Your Customer You're sophisticated. You make money. So it's time for your business to adjust its systems, particularly marketing and sales, to work the way your customers operate, to take the accidental customer "friction" out of your business.
		Part Five: An Easier, Simpler, More Profitable Business If you're going to go it alone, make sure you have these final elements to create what you really want…an easier, simpler, more profitable business.

TABLE 2: FOCUS AREAS		
Business Owner with Contractor Team	One-person business (You) supported by contractor team members; making between $150K and as much as you can	**Part One: Gain The Customertopia Mindset** You're rockin' it. Yet, that mind of yours holds you back, tells you lies and makes you believe you can achieve less than is within your reach. Master that devil! It's your first step on the road to Customertopia.
		Part Two: Think Like Your Customer You know you're supposed to build a customer-centered business. You've read that in all sorts of places, and you've made efforts. Part Two show you how to make very BEST efforts that change your results.
		Part Three: Act Like Your Customer This will be one of two very key sections of the book for you. You've always had elements of thinking like your customer but haven't always known or remembered to implement that thinking. Now you know. And precisely how.
		Part Four: Build For Your Customer This just might be the section of the book that breaks your business wide open, in a good way. Think like your customer. Check. Act like your customer. Check. Your biggest transitional behavior is likely upgrading your business into a customer-friendly system/process, eliminating random processes and replacing them with systematic marketing and sales systems/processes.
		Part Five: An Easier, Simpler, More Profitable Business Now your business should run like a well-oiled machine. Your next step is a well-oiled machine with additional support to turn it into an easier, simpler and more profitable business for you and your team.

TABLE 2: FOCUS AREAS		
Business Owner with Employees	Multi-person business; making over $500K	**Part One: Gain The Customertopia Mindset** On the surface there would appear to be little you need in the way of mindset adjustment. Yet, most of us do no matter how successful we are. Perhaps because you're successful already this will actually be a bit of hard work. No worries. You are not going to undo any of the magnificent success you've already had. You're adding to it.
		Part Two: Think Like Your Customer Yes, this section might be showing you some things you know. But are you putting them in place every day, in everything you do? Think like your customer and your business gets easier and more profitable, too.
		Part Three: Act Like Your Customer You're putting what you know about your customer into action. And, you might be experiencing a little business disruption. Trust us. When you learn to act like your customer wants, you'll unjam any customer acquisition logjams you might have or suspect you have.
		Part Four: Build For Your Customer Take a breath. You're going to be adjusting some of the marketing and sales systems/processes you have been using for years. We're asking you to do that because we know...know...these adjustments will move you into Customertopia.
		Part Five: An Easier, Simpler, More Profitable Business And here's your big pay-off...you're about to end feeling overwhelmed, of all roads leading to your desk and phone. Here's where someone (us) steps up and has your back.

ABOUT THE BOOK'S AIDS AND TOOLS

You'll find special features highlighted to assist you in building a Customertopia for you and your business. Overall the goal is an easy, and thought-provoking read. There are features in the book that provide additional sources of information and inspiration, or they challenge your preconceived ideas. Here's a list of features so you can watch for them or seek them out specifically.

Ah Ha Moments ⚡ share stories about our clients who have had...well... Ah Ha Moments using the Customertopia principles. These are examples of the most significant and pivotal points in the business owner's career. You'll see what split their mind open and enabled them to leap up a level, maybe several. Our Ideal Customers certainly had nervous moments and even fears as they looked at our recommendations. And then their Ah Ha arrived. Oh, boy. Did it arrive!

Sales Sidebars model specific sales strategies for you, but in this case, we're telling you how we are selling you when we're doing it so you can learn to do it for yourself. Yes, we might be evil, but more like evil geniuses as this transparency creates the best way to teach and sell at the same time! We do this in our presentations as well (see, this is us planting the seed we speak, and when you are ready to have an easier, simpler, more profitable business, you'll think of us). We could quote Confucius or Jay Conrad Levinson or some other insightful person, but when we quote ourselves, we become the expert in your mind.

Coaches' Questions enable you to focus on some of your main goals. These pose a question or two and provide some feedback on what you need to think about to gain the most from the information.

Coaching Exercises are meant for you to use over and over again. As you focus more carefully and thoughtfully on your business, your answers to the questions will evolve over time. You might find your goals change, too. Do these exercises, and you'll not only know, you'll also do.

Website-based Reference Tools provides useful book support tools you should download and use as you construct your Customertopia and use in your planning and implementation of your new approach. You'll find these special pages under the "Book Buyer" section of our website (https:// wideawakebusiness.com/resources). There you'll find all the worksheets and tools referenced in *Customertopia*, along with some special offers. You'll find our website to be a wealth of useful insights and tools, along with our blog and social media sites, to gather more advanced thoughts and seek advice and share ideas with your colleagues. Go to https://wideawakebusiness.com/resources and click on the Book Buyer button (yellow button).

Ready? We are. Let's get rolling.

COACHING EXERCISE 1: *Getting Ready*

Becoming a customer-centered, customer-first business will require some adjustments and changes to your business and life. Nothing scary. Some preparation is required. Also, not scary, sort of like planning and prepping dinner for your family. On non-McDonald's nights.

Ask yourself the following questions and write your honest answers. Make a deal with yourself to just let it all hang out even if it looks ugly...or immaculately beautiful. After all, if you can't trust yourself to create a little honesty, who can you trust?

1. I believe my biggest stumbling blocks in connecting with prospects is...

_____

_____

_____

_____

_____

_____

2. How much longer am I willing to operate in my business as it is?

_____

_____

_____

_____

_____

3. The business I yearn for really looks like this…

_____

_____

_____

_____

_____

_____

_____

4. Is this really what I want? Why? Am I ready now?

_____

_____

_____

5. Is my family willing to support this?

_____

_____

6. What do my prospects and customers tell me they want, and I'm not really listening to their request?

_____

_____

_____

_____

7. What do I talk to prospects about when I first speak with them? For example, my products and services, my credentials or something else?

_____

_____

_____

_____

8. What is the root reason why I drive myself to the point of being overwhelmed, exhausted and stressed?

_____

_____

_____

_____

9. What is my reason for not hiring more team to support my workload?

_____

_____

_____

_____

10. Am I doing most of the business work myself, managing my team or leading it…most of the time?

Look at your answers. If your answers clearly point to some things that must be addressed and fixed, let's fix them. If your answers indicate you're driving yourself to the point of being overwhelmed, you're about to see how to change that.

Tough questions, yes. And just to be totally upfront with you, there's a lot more to come.

Remember you will also find these exercises in a workbook, Customertopia Workbook and Planning Resource, on our website (wideawakebusiness.com/resources).

PART ONE

Gain The Customertopia Mindset

Coaches' Question: What stories does your mind tell you over and over again? You know, the stories it tries to get you to believe that really aren't true? Like you're not good enough, or smart enough or don't have enough experience for someone to spend money with you. Or whatever your brain tells you. Write down the stories your mind tells you, and then answer this question: what's in it for you to believe the story...because there is something in it for you. Otherwise, you wouldn't believe the story.

We all have that little voice in our heads telling us untrue stories, sometimes to protect us somethings just because that's what its job is. To move into Customertopia will require a transformation I how you think and act about your business, about your customer.

Acentral tenant of creating or moving your business into Customertopia requires you to have the ability to accept customers into your business. Sounds a bit strange to hear that rattle around in your head as you read it. What business owner wouldn't want to accept customers into their business with open arms! Yet, you're going to be surprised by all the things you are doing to send possible customers away.

Customertopia…accepting all the customers you want into your business…requires you to be "conditioned" for success. To run a marathon,

A CUSTOMERTOPIA PREREQUISITE IS CONDITIONING.

you must put longer and longer practice runs on your shoes. Biking a century race (100 miles) requires more than a bit of prep. The same is true for you to move your business to Customertopia. Conditioning is required.

If you've been successful in other endeavors, then you're going to understand the process required to create your Customertopia, and you'll make the move easily. If you've always struggled with building your business and making it a profitable endeavor, then it's time to take a look at your mindset as it might be the source of your struggle. And struggle will continue to haunt you until you transformed your attitude.

REORIENT YOUR MIND
AND YOUR BUSINESS APPROACH

One of our former clients, Marilyn King, was an Olympic athlete who shared an amazing story with us. Marilyn is a two-time Olympian, Munich in 1972 and Montreal in 1976. Her event was the grueling, demanding, painful Pentathlon, 10 track-and-field events requiring skill across a wide breadth of events. Marilyn decided she was all in to compete in the 1980 Olympics and quit her job…her source of income…in order to train every day, 24/7. One day while out training she was hit by a car, an accident that didn't seem serious at the time as she got up and walked away. But the next day her back went out like someone just twisted her in two different directions. The injury was misdiagnosed, and her pain increased, shooting from her head to her heels.

Two weeks go by. Three. Six. Nothing has changed. Yet, Marilyn was determined to make the team despite her pain impeding her ability to train. She knew she had to do something. She got films of the world record holders in all five of her events—hurdles, shot put, high jump, long jump and 800 meters. She watched them frame-by-frame and slow motion. She imagined herself doing exactly the same performances as these world record holders. She watched the videos day after day for weeks until she was sick of looking at them. So she went out on the track and imagined her performance...imagined it...envisioning "I will be in the top three in the Olympic Trials, and I'm getting better every day."

The Trial date arrives. Marilyn is still in pain. She's imagined her performance. She's seeing herself making the top three, the only athletes chosen to go to the Games. She hasn't actually run, hurdled, shot put or jumped in months. She hasn't participated in any events leading up to the Trials. Her fellow competitors wondered what had happened to Marilyn. On the day of the Trials she just showed up.

MARILYN OVERCAME HER PAIN AND WON BECAUSE SHE CONDITIONED HER MIND.

She placed second and made the team.

Marilyn pulled off this stunning achievement because, in her opinion, she conditioned her mind.

She created a vision. When her body was ailing, her mind took over. Marilyn's life transformed. She had considered herself a slightly above average athlete, and yet despite pain, despite an inability to train on the track, she made the Olympic team.

Marilyn now calls this Olympian thinking.

We call it completely mind-altering awesome...and a tremendous example of what we're all capable of achieving when we condition our mind to everything possible within us.

Your thoughts flow like a river traveling the same route day-after-day, week-after-week, year-after-year. The river has worn away the ground, creating a valley. Rock has smoothed, creating a path of least resistance. The water will continue to follow this path forever unless something changes.

Bring out the dynamite.

It's time to blow up the old path to craft a new one of your choice.

The river represents your thought patterns. Basically, you think the way you've always thought. Perhaps you don't believe you deserve a more successful business or that customers come easily to you. Perhaps you don't buy into the fact you don't need to work your fingers to the bone in order to earn the living you want. As long as you think those things, those things will be true.

Many of us were raised with conversations like "it takes hard work to succeed," or some other expression providing us with no positive enforcement. Statements like those increase the force of your river and cause the river to plow a deeper valley. But then something, or someone, comes along and plants a seed that begins to change your attitudes, your beliefs. You say "No more! I am going to build my business. I'm not messing around anymore. I really can grow to the next level and do it without breaking my back, without all roads leading to me." You mean what you said, yet your river continues to push you through the same path, down the same valley. You find yourself floundering in the same state of struggle.

What do you do?

You become Marilyn.

You recondition your mind like Marilyn, like you're a Pentathlon athlete training for the Olympics. You're going to build a dam to block that river from its usual, unacceptable flow. You're going to reroute the water, redirect your thoughts and beliefs about what can be achieved.

Super idea. But how do you do this?

We're not mind-set experts ourselves, but we sure know people who are. Here are some people to turn to discover methods that will work for you. Martha's favorite books come from Wayne Dyer. Check out his *Power of Intention* book. Chris loves *Mindset* by Carol Dweck. Many other mindset books await you. These are just two of our favs. One of our other favorite methods of reconditioning comes from relaxation tapes. Listening to positive statements about wealth, business success and personal development, and listening to them over and over, can start to build your dam to reroute your thought patterns towards what's really possible for you. More than you've believed or achieved to this point in your business.

ASK BETTER QUESTIONS

Our personal experiences over our past 12 years living Wide Awake Business, including business ups and certainly downs, have given us tools to transform our mind-set several times over. Yet, even recently we realized we were still playing small despite our success. We could see our colleagues and associates building healthy high six figures…seven figures…businesses, and we were not. So we made a decision. Stop limiting ourselves. Why shouldn't we have a bigger team to take over some of the work we were doing? Why couldn't we pay ourselves more? We began asking ourselves this question: Who do we want to become?

As it turned out, creating and delivering a live, in-person leadership retreat for women business owners provided our answer. Making this decision and doing the work to craft it was an explosion to our business, blowing open the doors to not just new revenue but also enabling us to see the unseen possibilities in our business. "Who do we want to become" opened our minds and our business.

WHO DO YOU WANT TO BECOME?

Ask yourself great questions, better questions, maybe some questions you've been afraid to ask or say out loud. Outstanding, unusual, tough questions offer a key to unlocking your yet-to-be-achieved goals. The question "How can I accelerate my business to half a million dollars?" or "What must I do to top $1 Million dollars this year" won't have the same power as "What haven't I thought of yet?" Martha asks a lot of questions. Sometimes it drives Chris a bit over the edge. Yet, our personal experience shows great questions deliver surprising answers, answers that will bend your river away from the same as always.

To start rerouting your mind river's path, you must be able to first, know there is another path, and then see the new path.

You must know what your business success looks like. Try **Coaching Exercise 3, A Day In Your Life Five Years From Now,** a bit farther along in this section. If you don't know what your goal looks like, how can you achieve it? Remember…think big! (no…bigger than that)

STAY STILL AND LISTEN

Customertopia might start as a mindset, one leading and guiding your business decisions by recognizing everything…everything…you do places your Ideal Customer in the heart of your business. Everything you create, describe, communicate, market, sell and support. With your Ideal Customer as the centerpiece you'll discover they come to you more easily. As they arrive without the stress and overwhelming feeling you might have now, you'll begin to make more money. And as you make more money,

CUSTOMERTOPIA
STARTS AS A
MINDSET.

you'll feel less stress which will enable you to create a business more people are attracted to (who is
attracted to work with a business that conveys stress
and crankiness?). With more money, not only will
you pay yourself more, you'll be able to hire more
team, contractors or employees. All the things you
want to do each day and fewer (maybe none) of the
things you don't want to do becomes yours.

What's perfect for you? Here are just a few questions to help you see
something unseeable right now:

COACHING EXERCISE 2: Questions to Open Your Mindset

1. On a scale of 1–10, with 10 being the highest, what does my "10 Life"
   look like, in detail?

   _____

   _____

   _____

2. On a scale of 1–10, with 10 being the highest, what does my Ideal Customer's 10 Life look like AFTER they have worked with me?

   _____

   _____

   _____

3. What work, that I'm not doing now, delivers higher value to my business? Higher value to my Ideal Customer?

   _____

   _____

   _____

4. How much time do I want to spend away from my office and how can I make this seamless?

_____

_____

_____

5. How big, revenue-wise, do I want my business to be?

_____

_____

_____

6. What's my very best-Case Study, one where my Ideal Customer's transformation was exceptional…and totally possible for others?

_____

_____

_____

7. When you solve your Ideal Customer's first problem…the one they have when they first come to you…what's the new problem they now have (they do have a new problem; it's the nature of the beast as you cannot solve all their issues in one product or program because they cannot absorb that much knowledge or change.)?

_____

_____

_____

8. What new product or program can you create that solves their "new" problem?

_____

_____

_____

Ask these questions and any others percolating for you. Then be still. Listen for the answers that bubble up. Don't force answers. That's your river trying to take over. Outlaw the same answers as always. Let your mind be free to the unexpected, the unusual, the often rejected.

When you give your mind permission to wander, to consider, to create it's going to hand you some surprises. A few surprises will be pleasant, and you'll be warmed by their arrival. Some revelations will seem foreign, maybe even impossible or ridiculous. Are they? Do not reject them right now. Just "be" with them. They will reveal their true potential, their true nature and applicability for you, in time. Other surprises will overwhelm you, cause you to gasp. Take a breath, write them down and say "Thank you" to your brain for letting them slip out.

Remember you are replotting your river. Your mindset river loves its ingrained path. However, you are not the river. You are so much more than that. When you ask great questions, then be quiet and listen you're going to be stunned by the alternative paths that reveal themselves.

....

COACHING EXERCISE 3: A Day In Your Life (Business and Personal) Five Years From Now

You may want to type out this exercise and save it. We'll be referring back to it a few times. Once you're finished, post it somewhere prominent and look at it regularly. Remember Marilyn, our Olympic athlete. She won her Olympic trial solely through visualization. So it must work, not only for her, but you also.

Go back to **A Typical Business Day in the Life of a Customertopia Business Person** (page 7) and read it again. Look at the verbs used...all present tense. Now write down what your perfect day looks like five years from now. Put down all the details.

What does your Ideal Customer look like? What do they aspire to? What problem keeps them from reaching their aspiration? What is the opportunity, the transformation, working with you enables them to achieve? How do you describe your business to new prospects? What customers do you speak to today? What services do you discuss? What is the fee for you to work together? Who on your team will do the work? What are you doing this day in addition to speaking with that customer? How does it feel to have your team delivering what is sold? What do your home and office life look like? How many team members do you have and what work are they doing for you? Who are your best Affiliate partners and how do you work together? Are they employees or contractors? How much revenue have you brought in on this Typical Day? What kind of fun are you having with family and friends? What does your health look like and your daily exercise routine?

Do not leave out the details...this is your perfect day. You want to describe it in such detail you can see it, feel it and taste it.

Once you have completed the exercise below, place it in a prominent place and review it every day for a month. What else do you now see and should be added to your Day? After a month, your description will be very complete. Now read it daily. Yes, I said very day. Make it a part of your morning ritual: Get up. Let the dogs out. Kiss the spouse. Make a cup of coffee. Read your **A Typical Business Day in the Life of a Customer-Centered Business Person**.

A TYPICAL BUSINESS DAY IN THE LIFE OF ME, A CUSTOMER-CENTERED BUSINESS PERSON

_____

_____

_____

_____

_____

_____

_____

_____

_____

_____

_____

_____

_____

_____

_____

_____

As you're writing your five-year vision, do not let the gremlins in! Your gremlin is the little, nasty, negative guy sitting on your shoulder saying things like "You're crazy. You can't do that!" Or "You've tried that, and it doesn't work." He could say "That's not even possible on your best day. Who are you kidding?" Your gremlin wants to herd you back to your river, to put limits on you. Do not let your gremlin drive the bus! Be in charge of yourself, of envisioning your business as you see it and want it—don't hold back.

Now go back to your five-year vision you just wrote or typed out. Make sure you're not playing small.

Remember you will also find these exercises in a workbook, Customertopia Workbook and Planning Resource, on our website (wideawakebusiness.com/resources).

PART TWO

Think Like Your Customer

Coaches' Question: What's encouraged you to be in business for your-self? What motivates you to get up every day and make money for yourself, your team, your family?

If you answer something like, "I have a unique ability to solve a prob-lem for certain people," then you're on to something. You're on the right track. Your statement focuses on your customer, particularly the most important thing putting them in motion. Solving their problem. This section of Customertopia will refine your approach to their problem. If you answered something other than that, this section of enable you to understand the importance of flipping your point-of-view to that of your Ideal Customer to grow your business, and do it in an easier, simpler and more profitable way. Frankly, any number of reasons motivated you to get into this business of yours. Your passion for what your talent can do for people will pull you through the tough days, coupled with perseverance to plow forward. The goal of Customertopia is to show you the step-by-step path to reduce the frequency of tough days and replace them with happier days. Be sure your motivation and commitment carry you to your long-term vision and desire.

KNOW THY CUSTOMERS

Your customers don't think like you.

Swaddle yourself in this blanket of truth, and you've taken a first, big step towards Customertopia.

Therefore, there's an undesirable and unintentional distance between your Ideal Customer and you.

Before we talk about how your customers really think, your reasoning process must be examined. When you understand how you think and talk about your product or service offering, you'll begin to see and understand the differences as we lay out how your Ideal Customer thinks and, therefore, acts. A roll-back in time to the first day you started your business will aid your understanding of how the distance between you and your Ideal Customer came about in the first place.

YOUR CUSTOMERS DON'T THINK LIKE YOU.

Stroll back to the very first day you decided to go into business for yourself. When you started your business, you chose a subject you understood very well, or perhaps a particular field called to you. You went to college, university, graduate school or attended a specialty program. Maybe you have none of that. Instead, you have years and years of life experience in your area of expertise.

No matter how you got where you are, here you are, an expert. You know much more about your subject than almost any of the customers with whom you are working or will serve.

Therefore, you think like an expert. You use the professional, expert language cultivated by your field (think about how your doctor speaks with you when you go in for an examine; you probably understand less than you'd prefer). That's what experts do. They use the language of their profession. Your education and training mean your Ideal Customer's problem and the solution to their problem isn't a mystery to you. You know precisely what your Ideal Customer *needs*. Consequently, you set about to fabricate the perfect, needed product or service, built to the specifications you've so laboriously sweated to create. You spend days, weeks, months… maybe even years…developing just the right thing you know your future customers really, really need.

Your Ideal Customer knows none of that.

Your Ideal Customer likely has no formal background in your area of expertise. Not only are they not an expert in your field, they might have no knowledge of your area. When they listen to you or visit your website, your use of professional language skidders away without creating a connection. Your rapid descent into a discussion about your product or service...because your product or service really, really delivers what they need...sounds like the teacher in the Charlie Brown cartoons. Wah, wah, wah.

YOUR IDEAL CUSTOMER LIKELY HAS NO BACKGROUND IN YOUR AREA OF EXPERTISE.

You're marketing and selling your service using with all the professionalism your education and wisdom have created. Yet, little-to-nothing happens.

You just told your Ideal Customer *everything important*...to you. You fervently and earnestly communicated all the stunning features they need to solve their problem. You shared your background, who you are and why you're so passionate about your product or service. How could they not buy from you? You're perfect for them!

Your Ideal Customer didn't hear a word.

You didn't talk to them about what's on *their* mind.

You talked to them about what's on *your* mind.

You used your very professional language which they don't have, don't understand and cannot hear.

Your Ideal Customer doesn't think like you.

They don't care about you. They don't care about your service.

They care about themselves.

They care about solving their problem, the one they believe they have. They care about taking away the headache keeping them from wherever they want to go. They care about making their life better, happier and richer.

Based on what you've shared, they have no idea you understand their problem. Therefore, no connection happens.

Your Ideal Prospect fails to become your Ideal Customer.

Your Ideal Prospect heads out in search of the someone who *gets* them.

Yet, your Ideal Prospect will stick to you like gum on a shoe once they begin to *hear you and recognize you understand their problem, rather than you understand a solution.*

Problem recognition comes first. Understanding your Ideal Customer's problem requires a special point-of-view. Theirs rather than yours.

RECOGNITION OF THEIR PROBLEM COMES BEFORE RECOGNITION OF A SOLUTION.

Problem solving is, in the end, what your job is all about. Yet, many small business owners spend more of their time promoting their products, offering up their solutions and generally looking at the prospect from the owner's point-of-view.

Until the prospect understands we understand the problem they actively seek to solve, there's little opportunity to make any kind of connect to the solution.

Few care about the solution to their problem. As Chris often says, they don't care if we use mashed potato solutions or rain drop solutions. They just want to know we understand their problem. If we meet them where they are, they will be more than happy to listen and, likely, act.

Only then will they be willing to listen and devote the time required to understand your solution.

The business owner who first understands and shares the problem the Ideal Customer believes they have becomes the winner. The business owner

YOUR #1 BUSINESS REQUIREMENT IS TO HAVE INSIGHTS INTO THE MIND OF YOUR IDEAL CUSTOMER.

who first understands and shares the solution likely loses that opportunity every time.

When you have and use insights into the mind of your Ideal Customer, your business will turn. Your Ideal Prospects will lift their heads and perk up their ears. Insights into how your Ideal Customer thinks enable you to understand how your Ideal Customer feels and acts. Insights empower you to turn away from operating from your point-of-view in favor of being a customer-centered company where everything (really...everything) evolves from your Ideal Customer's perspective.

Wonderful! Let's go, you say. You're ready and anxious to nail down those insights. You want to begin to use them in your business and change your fortunes.

Rarely, will we ask you to slow down. Yet, we're going to do that now.

Resist the temptation to dive into figuring out your Ideal Customer's problem. A very important step comes before we go there.

First, before we nail down the problem, we must determine who your Ideal Customer truly is.

THY CUSTOMER

Many small business owners haven't stopped to think deeply about who their very best customer might be. We call them your Ideal Customer because they are simply perfect for you.

Many business owners describe their Ideal Customer as "anybody who" or "everybody who..."

That doesn't narrow the field, does it?

Unless you have a very gigantic marketing budget, a team of sales people at the ready and a highly common problem you solve, "anybody who" and "everybody who" creates a playing field so broad you'll never be able to reach or develop it.

When you say, "anybody who…" the word anybody could be exchanged for somebody, and somebody tells you nothing about who you're seeking. Anybody indicates you haven't thought very much about your customer. Anybody means you're pursuing business from whomsoever flashes a little cash or credit card. Perhaps you feel willing to work with "anybody who" because you're in need of revenue. But are they the right Ideal Customer for you, and are you the right problem-solver for them? Too often the "anybody will do" kinds of clients turn into problems, not because the person is a problem rather because they just aren't right for you. Instead, exchange "anybody who…" for a specific profile of Ideal Customer in order to grow. You must identify and develop a smaller, tightly defined Ideal Customer in order to attract business.

If you say, "everybody who…," everybody really means "ya'll come." The world and every person in it can use your service. Let's assume for one lonely little minute that it's true. Every person in the world could use your service. How will you reach them all? Is your marketing budget so exceptionally large you can afford to mass market to the masses because "everyone" means everyone? And everyone means mass market. And mass market means big spending. Because mass market means competing with the very biggest guys in your field, and their pockets of spending and influence for deep.

Many business owners experience a shiver at the idea of narrowing who they seek for business. Their brow furrows when we lay the requirement on the table. They wring their hands, concerned they will miss out on business, that people with money to spend won't spend it with them. They believe casting the very widest net brings the most business.

Nothing could be farther from the truth.

Let me borrow from Seth Godin who wrote an entire book, *Small is the New Big*, begging you to appeal to a niched customer. Small is your new big. When you concentrate on a small segment of the entire market available to you (the "anybody who" and "everybody who" market), you rise above all the market noise and are heard. Your empathy for your Ideal Customer's problem can be seen, heard and appreciated. You no longer are a voice yelling in the great wild.

CUSTOMERTOPIA REQUIRES A THOUGHTFUL EXAMINATION OF YOUR BEST CUSTOMER.

Even if you've been in business for decades chances are great you haven't given much thought to the profile of your Ideal Customer, or dusted it off and updated it based on this new world we all live and operate in. If you have your Ideal Customer profile identified perfectly, have you written it down? Shared it with your team? Writing down your Ideal Customer profile creates an anchor for you as you seek them. Their profile bakes into your bones. You'll never forget and drift. On the other hand, when the profile rambles around in your head without the anchoring of writing, the profile will morph, float or be forgotten in favor of the person standing in front of you flashing some Ben Franklins.

Customertopia—the place you want to move where your business becomes easier, simpler and more profitable—requires a thoughtful examination of your best customer, your Ideal Customer.

You're going to replace "anybody who" and "somebody who" for someone quite specific.

THE REWARD FOR SACRIFICE

As we work together to accurately identify your Ideal Customer, there will be certain types of potential customers outside that description. Certain profiles of potential customers will be left behind for others to serve. You will not be speaking to them directly.

Did a shiver just shimmy down your spine? The hairs on your arms stand up at attention at the thought of serving only a fragment of your potential audience?

Painting the specific and accurate picture of your very best customer necessitates an act of sacrifice on your part.

In choosing *someone* you'll be eliminating someone. Often many someones.

AH HA MOMENT 🗲 : ALISON

Several years ago, we worked with a mid-30s financial planner to identify her Ideal Customer. Our client, Alison, was a young woman with a husband of 10 years and two children under the age of eight. Her financial planning business produced acceptable results. But she didn't want acceptable. She wanted lively, sparkling and invigorating. Alison busied herself marketing in pursuit of working with "everybody." While highly talented in her field, Alison wasn't earning what she wanted for the time she invested in her business. She wanted to contribute more money to the family coffers and pay for many of her children's educational expenses. The thought of narrowing her "best" Ideal Customer profile gave her pause. She fretted she'd be bringing in less money, not more.

We had several long conversations with Alison, and she completed several assignments at our request. Her Ideal Customer became obvious, at least to us. Her Ideal Customer was a young family with kids under the age of 15. She knew those families perfectly. She had done quite a bit of work with younger families. Alison understood their unique challenges at this early stage of their saving for the future. What they wanted to accomplish diverged substantially from a person seeking to retire in 10 years. Alison's Ideal Customer profile identified they had two incomes to support their family, and they didn't have a single dollar to waste on the wrong investments. She appreciated young families had budgets yanked in many different and unexpected directions—school, clothing, sports, Mom's and Dad's taxi service and more. Alison knew what the real life of a young family looked like. She respected their near and long-term goals for investing.

Could any other customer profile be more perfect?

We were convinced Alison's very best Ideal Customer comprised young families with children under the age of 10.

Alison's fretting grabbed her hard. Her brows knitted together. Her smile stretched to a grimace. What about all the other people she had served, she wanted to know? How could she just toss back "everybody" who approached her for retirement planning and other needs? Doing that would cut her business back, not enable it to grow. She was certain.

We talked to her about the fact this step was a choice—she could trial the new Ideal Customer and marketing approach or stick with what she was doing (that wasn't getting the results she wanted). We shared she had to be "all in." This was a move to flirt with. Dedication was demanded.

Alison was willing to push aside her nervousness. She agreed to give it a shot. A shot or a full commitment, we asked. Alison agreed to put her all into attracting this Ideal Customer. But she was only willing to dedicate herself to it for six months. If it wasn't working after six months, Alison was heading back to "everyone."

Flash forward six months. Alison's financial services business had grown by 32%. Of course, she kept all the customers with whom she was already working, including the ones who didn't fit her new profile. Her biggest discovery came when she looked at how many new customers she had fitting her Ideal Customer profile and the amount of money they had invested through her. While individually they had less money to invest than her "everybodys", she had attracted many more young clients than ever before. By identifying a specific Ideal Customer and accurately discussing the problem they believed they had...as her Ideal Customer saw it...Alison attracted new business from young families to grow by 32%.

Certainly, people who didn't fit her Ideal Customer profile occasionally approached her to work together. Alison accepted their business when it was right for them and right for Alison. She didn't turn them away, and you won't either when it happens to you.

Ten years later Alison's business continues to expand. She's brought on two financial advisors to work with her. Moms and Dads of young families at the early stage of building their financial future represent over 75% of her business. Alison attributes every smidgen of this growth to her willingness to end her "anyone who" and "everyone who" approach to her business in favor of speaking to a very specific Ideal Customer.

The same burst of wonderfulness will happen to you, too, when you become specific about who your Ideal Customer really is. The best Ideal Customer. The one you're excited to attract, see and serve.

Coaches' Question: *Who are you willing to sacrifice? Which Ideal Customer profile brings you the most revenue and happiness? How much do they spend with you in total...everything that Ideal Customer profile buys from you on average? Now you know how valuable they are to you and your business. This is your reward for sacrifice.*

HOW TO IDENTIFY YOUR IDEAL CUSTOMER

You must be open to a bit of navel-gazing to identify your very best Ideal Customer, along with some sifting and sorting as there's more to recognizing them than just a few demographic characteristics. You're going to create your Ideal Customer profile by examining them through four prisms.

1. Their demographic, psychographic and behavior profile

2. Their built-in, already existing buying motivators

3. Their aspiration in your area of expertise

4. The problem they *actively want* to solve

When Chris talks to our Wide Awake Business customers about identifying their Ideal Customer, she tells them to think like they are looking for customers "wearing orange socks." Your Ideal Customer profile might not have anything to do with socks, not to mention orange ones. But the profile you create will be that specific. Well, almost.

YOUR IDEAL CUSTOMER PROFILE

Your identification of your very best Ideal Customer begins with an examination of who they are. You're going to identify the demographics and behavior setting them apart from the rest of the people you could serve... but will not.

You'll identify your Ideal Customer by looking at these demographics:

- Age & Generation
- Gender
- Income Level
- Location
- Race or Ethnicity
- Education

- Marital Status
- Type of Business (if your Ideal Customer is a business rather than a consumer)
- Title (again, if your Ideal Customer is a business)

Some or all these demographics will be a part of your Ideal Customer profile. For example, if your business operates using the Internet, location might be eliminated as relevant. The Internet can generate Ideal Customers from just about anywhere on the globe. If, on the other hand, you have a physical office, location becomes a critical component of your Ideal Customer profile.

Please pay particular attention to the age/generation and income attributes as they will provide greater insights into your Ideal Customer. Age and generation become important since how your Ideal Customer gathers information changes markedly based on their age and generation. Martha used to walk her pup around her neighborhood on Sunday mornings and would see a newspaper resting in the driveway. She knew a Baby Boomer or older person lived in that house. She knew that because Baby Boomers and elders still read a physical newspaper. If your Ideal Customer was a Baby Boomer, you could use a newspaper ad to attract their attention. On the other hand, if you want to attract a Millennial, the newspaper would be the wrong place for you to spend your marketing dollars. Millennials might read a newspaper, but they'll read it on-line. If your Ideal Customer was a Millennial, you could use the on-line newspaper to attract their attention.

Income must be examined under the light of how much your services cost. Your Ideal Customer must have an income capable of paying for your services. We watch too many small business owners seek individuals who cannot pay for the services, often because the business owner's heart gets mixed with their wallet. Whether the small business owner does this out of nervousness (they want to be open to "anybody who" or "everybody who) or out of charity (they feel great empathy for people who cannot afford the solution they need...which is really charity, not a paying Ideal Customer), income must be aligned to an ability to pay.

• • • • • • • • • • • • • • • • • **SALES SIDEBAR**

Now why on earth do we tell you about paying attention to what people can afford to pay you? Two reasons:

1. We want you to understand from the very first step you'll be using these insights to bring in new customers...to sell more people on your services.

2. We're doing what all of you should be doing when you talk to people using their insights...planting seeds. We build your sales processes with you. It's one of the things we do very, very well. We want you to know everything going on in our world, so you'll want to buy what we offer (we're more than just pretty faces, after all!)

Next, you'll observe your Ideal Customer's psychographics, the classification of your Ideal Customer based on attitudes, activities and opinions.

Before we utter another word about psychographics, please read the next sentence. *These attitudes, activities and opinions have nothing to do with you.* You are not examining their attitudes about you or their opinions about your services. You are not exploring the reasons they tell you they cannot work with you. At this stage, your Ideal Customer doesn't know you exist. The attitudes, activities and opinions you're seeking to uncover belong to your Ideal Customer as they understand the field in which you operate.

For example, if you're a business coach, your Ideal Customer's attitudes, activities and opinions about coaching might be rooted in the fact they've used a coach in the past (and have a positive attitude). They believe business owners serious about their business should use a coach (has an opinion). Plus, they willingly find time on their schedule to work with their coach and complete any assignments (will to be in action).

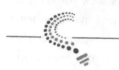

THE ATTITUDES, ACTIVITIES AND OPINIONS OF YOUR IDEAL CUSTOMER HAVE NOTHING TO DO WITH YOU.

Last, you'll examine their behaviors (again, not their behaviors with you) in your area of expertise. Behaviors include the way they act or conduct themselves. Examples of behavior could include such words as they find coaches to be caring, charming, considerate, enthusiastic, excitable, stress out, funny, faithful, irritable, dominate and the like. The behaviors you identify can be clustered into four areas: aggressive, assertive, passive and passive-aggressive.

Using demographics, psychographics and behaviors you will develop a distinct portrait of your precise Ideal Customer. Shortly, you'll find Coaching Exercises below to aid you in your work to reveal your very best Ideal Customer. These Coaching Exercises support you in your efforts to discover this information about your Ideal Customer.

If you're still scratching your head after completing the above Coaching Exercise, our next conversation will assist you in your work.

IF YOU'VE BEEN IN BUSINESS

For those of you who have been in business for a few years, the task of identifying your Ideal Customer shouldn't be difficult. You just require a sharp eye and filter.

First, begin by examining what your current customers look like. Are they mostly men or women? Mostly…remember working to filter out "everybody" and "anybody." Are they of a certain age? Do they live in a particular area of your town or the country? Is it important for them to live in your area, or not? How much money do they make (and they must make enough money to afford your services)? If you work with businesses, what's the title of the person with whom you want to work? What's the industry you work with most often, and enjoy?

When you examine your current customers closely, they will begin to cluster around a few profiles. Your existing customers have traits in common. Identify the traits and cluster them into profiles. You'll likely have more than one or two.

Next, look very closely at all those profiles. Some customers you like...a lot. You love working with that type of person or business. They love working with you. They grow and change. They're excited to work with you, and you with them. They pay on time.

Other customers might not be so wonderful. You took them because... well...because they said "yes." You knew you could solve their problem yet working with them was painful. Perhaps they complained or didn't do the things you told them. Their advancement amounted to little or nothing. Maybe they didn't pay on time or charged back through their credit card company.

One or two of your profiles you love and want more of them. Several profiles might be okay, but you didn't love the experience. Other profiles were flat-out painful, and if you didn't have to work with that type of customer anymore, that would be okay. Good news: when you identify your very best Ideal Customer, you don't have to work with the folks who gave you pain (and you likely gave them some agony, too).

Next, look at the one or two profiles you love. These people represent your very best Ideal Customers. If you had a whole business of that type of customer, you'd be as happy as an eagle soaring in the sky on a gorgeous summer evening. You're only choosing one, maybe two profiles. That's it. After that, you're wandering back into "anyone who..." and "everyone who" territory.

You've now found your Ideal Customer. Feels pretty good, doesn't it? Maybe a little scary, too.

You might feel a little scared right now as you're not going to pursue certain people you've worked with in the past and who spent money with you. They will no longer be the clients you seek. You can cease to market to them. You can turn them away graciously when they show up on their own. You can say "I'm happy to refer you to a colleague" because you have someone who loves the type of customer that's not for you.

You're going to question your decision to not work with that type of person when they show up. You're giving up revenue. Like Alison before you, you're about to discover that homing in on your very specific, very best Ideal Customer will actually enable your business to grow and grow more easily, simply and profitably.

. . . .
COACHING EXERCISE 4: *Identifying Your Ideal Customer*
If You've Been in Business for a Time

Ask yourself the following questions and write your honest answers. Make a deal with yourself to just let it all hang out even if it looks ugly...or immaculately beautiful. You know the answers. You do. Really.

1. As you've been in business for a time, identify the demographics, psychographics and behaviors of the customers who show up most frequently in your business. They look like this:

_____

_____

_____

_____

_____

2. What do you like about the customers showing up now? What don't you like?

_____

_____

_____

_____

3. Do you want more of that customer? Are they the right one for your business? Do you love working with this customer?

_____

_____

_____

_____

4. If this profile needs to be adjusted or completely overhauled so you are working with your very best Ideal Customer going forward, what is that profile by demographics, psychographics and behaviors?

_____

_____

_____

_____

IF YOU'RE JUST STARTING YOUR BUSINESS

For those of you just starting your business or with limited experience, identifying your Ideal Customer might feel like looking for the light switch in a blacked-out room. You haven't had enough customers to know who's best.

What you perceive as bad news...you have little-to-no customers to aid you in your discovery of their profile...becomes the good news. You have a clean slate with which to work. Unlike people in business for years who must identify their best from many profiles and clear their plate of those who no longer fit, you don't have to do any of that. Your clean slate means you can choose.

You don't have anything to clean up or eliminate. You get to identify the right Ideal Customer right from right now.

Therefore, here's the very most important question for you to ask yourself and answer:

Who do you want?

What are the demographic, psychographic and behavior traits of the customer you'd love to work with? Choose. Just choose.

CHOOSING SOMEONE DELIVERS RESULTS SUPERIOR TO CHOOSING EVERYONE.

Did you just get a little nervous because you cannot figure out how to choose? Do you feel you don't have enough info to be anything other than dangerously wrong? And what if you choose incorrectly. Everything could be wrong, wrong, wrong from Day One!

Here's the thing about choosing, *choosing someone whether they are the right person or totally wrong person is infinitely better for you than "anyone who" or "everyone who..."*

As you get more experience, as you serve more people, you'll come back to this exercise and refine, refine, refine. You'll know more because you're now alert to the need to be observant, to not just say "yes" and take their money. You now will be watching who you love working with and who not so much. You'll know the type of person who works for their betterment and those who talk but don't do. You'll know who's tempting but the devil in disguise. You'll know.

....
COACHING EXERCISE 5: *Identifying Your Ideal Customer If You're Just Starting Your Business*

Ask yourself the following questions and write your honest answers. Make a deal with yourself to just let it all hang out even if it looks ugly...or immaculately beautiful. Give it your very best effort knowing you'll always be able to adjust as you get more experience and more customers.

1. As you're just starting your business, what are the demographics, psychographics and behaviors of the Ideal Customer you want?

   _____

   _____

   _____

2. What will you watch for in your Ideal Customer's demographics, psychographics and behaviors as you begin working with people? What will be your keys to adjust your Ideal Customer profile as you get more business experience?

   _____

   _____

   _____

Remember, all these Coaching Exercises are available
to you, along with special offers on our website:
wideawakebusiness.com/resources

YOUR IDEAL CUSTOMER BUYING MOTIVATORS

Good news arrives in many shapes and forms. Consider this section. This section of *Customertopia* contains nothing but fabulous news. *Very good news!*

We're going to show you a few easy and spectacular methods of discovering critical insights about your Ideal Customer. The insights you gather take the hard, complex and less profitable part of attracting the right people...your Ideal Customers...out of your business. Instead, you'll have the ability to create the very conversation your Ideal Customer seeks because that conversation enables them to see and hear you in very noise, crowded markets.

BUYING MOTIVATORS ARE ALREADY BUILT IN TO YOUR IDEAL CUSTOMER.

Good news #1: Your Ideal Customer, who you just identified, has their buying motivators already built in!

You don't have to convince, hypnotize or send your Ideal Customer some sort of subliminal message while they're sleeping. Think about that. If you slam on the breaks at the idea of reaching out to prospects to turn them into your Ideal Customer because you feel you have to "convince them" to work with you, you've just discovered you've been telling yourself a story.

Good news #2: You don't have to sort through hundreds of buying motivators to find the one perfect one just right for each of your Ideal Customers. Only two buying motivators exist, and only one will apply to every single one of your Ideal Customers.

One of two buying motivators live within your Ideal Customer driving them to act.

The first buying motivator drives your Ideal Customer to get rid of a problem. Think of it this way. They are living with a headache, and they want it gone!

They actively seek a remedy to their headache. They are not indifferent to their problem. They want it removed. They want their headache to go away. They are reacting to something undesirable. The odds are exception they don't know what will take away their headache. So they aren't looking at your solution or anyone else's solution. As a matter of fact, they aren't hunting for a solution at all because they don't know what solution takes away their headache. Research shows only 5% of all your Ideal Prospects believe they know the solution and are looking for that solution. Five percent! What are the other 95% doing? They are searching for answers, turning over boulders, inquiring of friends, digging through the Internet because they don't know what will take away the headache. When they have a headache, you become their aspirin. They just want to move away from pain, challenge, issue, dilemma—whatever word is appropriate. The sooner the better.

The second buying motivator propels your Ideal Customer to take something pretty good and make it even better. Their desire for something even better moves them forward to find what will create greater pleasure. People seeking to turn something good into something great are proactive rather than reactive. You'll find them in motion when things are good. They act with their eye to the future needs, perhaps heading off a problem before it even appears or accelerating today for an even more positive tomorrow. They, too, have no idea what the solution might be. All they know is this "thing" can get much better. They want to move towards gratification, towards pleasure, towards greater happiness or joy. When they want something better, you become their vitamin. The sooner the better.

Good news #3: Approximately 80% of your Ideal
Customers will, first, be in motion to solve their problem
rather than make something good even better.

Therefore, your odds of identifying your Ideal Customer's buying motivator shines. Your Ideal Customer seeks to solve a problem (let's just call it a problem; sure you might like…or they might like…challenge, issue or dilemma…better; we're going to use problem here because you know what? It likely is a problem). They have a headache. You become their aspirin.

Humans attend to their headaches before they step forward to make something better. Therefore, wrap yourself around the belief and likelihood that your Ideal Customer has a problem they want to solve. Now you know what drives them to buy. You probably didn't know that just a minute ago. Congrats.

• • • • • • • • • • • • • • • • **SALES SIDEBAR**

We just hopped off the phone with William, one of our top coaching clients. He's super aware of his business. He realized he's great at his CPA business, yet a bit challenged in taking the right steps to grow it. Like many business owners, William can put his head down and create amazing, honest tax returns that lower his clients' tax debts. But how to get more clients? That was a bigger challenge. In the past, the task of developing a marketing and sales plan would fall behind almost everything. This year he hired a coach (us) to develop his plan, identify his Very Best Ideal Customer and determine where he would go to find them. We nailed down his one, singular, measurable goal for the entire year...the one thing every task, effort, call, hire and system would be in place to deliver. Then we identified his four Critical Success Factors that must be in play all year to deliver that goal. He identified his goal and Critical Success Factors in 120 minutes rather than 120 days. Having a coach on your team delivers measurable value, doesn't it? You tell us.

This story might seem like a self-promotion. It is, and that's okay. We want you to think about your own weak links in your business and who you might grab to be a part of your team to support you to drive faster to your goal. If it's us, that's wonderful.

This is us asking for the business, sales 101. Are you asking for the business in your books, phone calls and speaking engagements?

Think about how these three enlightenments merge together, your Ideal Customer, their buying motivator and you. If they (your Ideal Customer) have a headache and a problem they want to solve (their buying motivator), you (also known as you) rise up to be their aspirin. If they are in a good space and they want to make it better, you become their vitamin.

You might be inclined to say your Ideal Customer seeks a vitamin. Your personal desire for your Ideal Customer bubbles over with good will and longing for their happiness. All of us want to make our Ideal Customer's life better. However, we ask you to stop for just a moment. We completely understand you want to deliver nothing but goodness, happiness, pleasure, gratefulness, success, joy, relaxation, contentment, glee, gladness, blessedness, laughter and peace of mind. You want that for your Ideal Customer. But is it what your Ideal Customer wants? Right now? As their first step?

Here's a real-life example from one of our Ideal Customers.

AH HA MOMENT ⚡: JANICE

Janice works with parents who want their child to stop throwing tantrums, yelling, slamming doors and talking back, the sort of tween behavior giving both the parent and child headaches. Janice's Ideal Customers weren't looking for an outcome that's vitamin-like. They weren't looking for a happy household. They were blinded to that possibility as it seemed so remote based on where they were at that moment. A happy household felt like an impossible day dream. Please just stop the tantrums, they would say. Yet, Janice marketed the return of a happy home. She wanted all her Ideal Customers to have smiles on their faces and for parents and kids to enjoy each other. Janice had her heart in the right place. We wanted a vitamin for her Ideal Customers.

Her Ideal Customer, on the other hand, couldn't stretch their vision to a happy home. They wanted the tantrums, yelling, slammed doors and talking back to end. Therefore, they couldn't hear or respond to Janice when she conveyed the outcome of working with her created a happy household. Her Ideal Customer's ears could only hear and relate to a business that created a household without tantrums, yelling, slammed doors and talking back. Janice resisted our recommendation to talk about eliminating the problem rather than delivering a happy home. She just couldn't see how a happy home (a vitamin) would be less valuable than eliminating the tantrums (the aspirin).

Janice persisted with her preferred approach...until her business stopped growing. Worse yet, she was rolling backwards without any response to her marketing. Janice felt her marketing was the issue, where she was marketing. She asked us to look. We did. Nothing was inherently off about the "where" she was marketing. Her message, on the other hand, attracted no attention. Now with her back against the proverbial financial wall, Janice was finally willing to make changes in how she attracted prospects. She changed all her Ideal Customer conversations (marketing and sales) to focus on putting an end to the terror in the house...tantrums, yelling (everybody's yelling, right), slammed doors and talking back. Slowly, her results began to improve, accelerated because she was speaking the language her Ideal Customer could hear and see. Guess what Janice says today? She creates homes without tantrums, yelling, slammed doors and back-talk, just what her Ideal Customers crave.

If you want your Ideal Customer to perk up their ears, turn their head towards you and shut out everything else, you must speak to the problem they believe they have. Janet's Ideal Customers were motivated to find a way to eliminate tantrums, yelling, door slamming and talking back. Why not tell them that's what she does?

Do you see the difference in that approach?

"I work with you to create a happy household."

"I work with you to fully eliminate tantrums, yelling, slammed doors and talking back."

If you had a misbehaving child, to which would you respond?

Your Ideal Customer operates just as Janice's do. Your responsibility means you will figure out which of the two built-in buying motivators exist already within your Ideal Customer. Then you'll speak to them in their language, how they convey their problem or pleasure to you. If they are looking for an aspirin, use aspirin language. If they are looking for a vitamin, use vitamin language.

Before we proceed to the next step in thinking like your customer, let's take just a moment to review what you've discovered so far:

- You now have a specific and identifiable profile of who your Ideal Customer is

- You no longer speak to "anyone who..." or "everybody who..."

- You know your Ideal Customer already has their buying motivators built-in; you never have to convince anyone to buy from you again

- Only two buying motivators exist...just two not hundreds to wade through and figure out

- One of those two buying motivators exists already within your Ideal Customers

- About 80% of your Ideal Customers are likely driven to action because they have a problem, one of the two buying drivers, they are actively engaged in solving

You see why we said this section of *Customertopia* was worth the entire price of the book? Look what you know now you didn't know just minutes ago! Look how much easier your life just become. We've just begun to scratch the surface of goodness.

HOW TO DETERMINE YOUR IDEAL CUSTOMER BUYING MOTIVATOR

Knowing only two built-in buying motivators makes for a simpler path to determine which of the two already lives within your Ideal Customer. However, we can smell your next worry from here: how do I figure out which of the two applies to my Ideal Customer?

ASK AND LISTEN.

Great question, and the answer resides in front of you. You...listen to your Ideal Customer. Whether they are currently your customer, a prospect you're developing or simply someone you'd like to work with, put yourself in their presence and ask some inquiring questions.

What's going on for you right now (in your area of expertise)?

How long have you been living with this issue?

What solutions have your tried to date?

If it doesn't get addressed...fixed...what will happen?

These types of questions, and more, enable you to unmask your Ideal Customer's built-in buying motivators. Ask and then listen. What did they say, and just as importantly, how did they say it? Write it down *exactly* as they expressed it to you. Don't change a word or convert it into your expert language. Are they speaking as though they have a headache? Or are they using language indicating they are searching for something better?

Listening provides the key to unearthing the insights you seek. Ask and listen. Isn't that easier than you thought it would be?

If you've been in business for a reasonable time, you have the opportunity to ask, ask, ask, listen and talk to your existing Ideal Customers to gather their thoughts about what's going on for them. As you listen, pay strict attention to the words they use. We call them the "Words of the Customer." You want to use those same words, rather than translate into your professional language. Your Ideal Customer easily hears what you're saying when you say it like they say it. They hear it and feel it when you use their words. When you translate to something, anything, other than their words, it makes it much more difficult for them to recognize you're talking to them.

If you're just starting your business and you feel you don't have enough customers presently to gather the information you need to nail down your Ideal Customer's buying motivator, you still have access to people who fit your Ideal Customer profile. Determine where your Ideal Customer currently "hangs out?" Can you talk to them at a Chamber meeting, share a coffee at an event or exchange messages on Facebook or LinkedIn? Don't be afraid to ask them questions. You're not selling them anything, at least not yet! You're gathering insights into the mind of your customer to understand what makes them tick, what moves them into action.

Coaches' Question: How strong are your listening skills? As you find yourself in the presence of your Ideal Customer, are you talking more than asking great questions and listening to their answers? Are you writing down what they've said, exactly as they've said it (when you're no longer in their presence, not in front of them!)? Ask a friend to role-play a sales conversation with you. How many great questions did you ask (a few, not tens)? What did they say? How accurate were you in writing down their responses? It takes practice to master the skill of listening. Practice.

COACHING EXERCISE 6: Determine Your Ideal Customer's Buying Motivator

Based on conversations you've had or will have with your Ideal Customer, write down their honest answers about what drives them. Remember: this isn't what encourages them to say "yes" to work with you. You're not in this conversation. All the answers below come from your Ideal Customer about what they want for themselves.

1. When you talk to your Ideal Customer about the problem/challenge/issue/dilemma they have (in your area of expertise...not with you), what do they say?

_____

_____

_____

2. Are they using aspirin or vitamin language?

_____

_____

_____

3. Now look at how you talk about your business on your website, brochures and the like. What are you talking about? Yourself? Your services? Or the problem and what happens when the problem goes away (no more yelling)?

_____

_____

_____

YOUR IDEAL CUSTOMER ASPIRATIONS

Look at the progress you've made. You know who your Ideal Customer is or have a pretty reasonable idea. You identified your Ideal Customer's built-in buying motivator and know how to articular it in your business.

Your third step in transforming your business to think like your customer means you're going to do some digging into what they aim to achieve in the area in which you operate.

Your Ideal Customer aspires to something (not their aspirations in working with you). They have a desire for something to happen, a hope that burns within.

They yearn for something. They have a dream, something real, totally possible. This is not a daydream or fantasy on their part. Your Ideal Customer's aspiration lives within them, and they actively strive to achieve, it. The dice roll in your favor when they don't know how to achieve it.

Understanding what your Ideal Customer seeks to achieve means you're taking the next step to gain insights into the mind of your Ideal Customer, to think like your Customer. When you have an precise understanding of their aspirations, you'll be able to speak their language in your marketing and sales. When you accurately comprehend and talk about where your Ideal Customer wants to go, their underlying aspirations, you provide your Ideal Customer with one more path to click into you through the din of a crowded, noisy market.

YOUR IDEAL CUSTOMER YEARNS FOR SOMETHING POWERFUL AND MOTIVATING.

HOW TO IDENTIFY YOUR IDEAL CUSTOMER'S ASPIRATIONS

Your Ideal Customer thinks and ponders their aspirations through two different, but aligned, expressions. Both expressions give you a peek into how they think and what they seek for themselves, family, health, wealth, business, spouse or other within the area you specialize in (not what they aspire to with you). Both expressions of their aspirations must be identified because, again, you want to use them in your business to enable your Ideal Customer to hear you in this loud, earsplitting world we live in. One of the two expressions is important to know; the other is critical.

Surface Aspirations showcase the basic ambitions your Ideal Customer seek. Surface aspirations can include desires such as more money, a shinier car, a healthier body, a safe environment for your elder Mom or the end of yelling. Surface aspirations ring completely true, and you must know them. Yet, bigger ambitions loom moving your Ideal Customer to action.

Deep and True Aspirations represent strong, emotional desires in your Ideal Customer. Deep and true aspirations deal with the heart of your Ideal Customer. Rarely are deep and true aspirations tangible. Instead, they are immaterial, nothing you can hold in your hand. Your Ideal Customer values their deep and true intangible aspirations more highly than the surface aspirations. Deep and true aspirations can include the desire to feel good about taking good financial care of the family, feeling better about how they take care of their health, so they are around for their kids, not worrying about Mom's health when they are miles away or experiencing the relief of tension in the family when the yelling subsides. Think of them as the true destination for which your Ideal Customer yearns.

Here's a real-world example of both surface and deep and true aspirations for you to use as a guidepost as you begin the process of identifying them in your Ideal Customer.

AH HA MOMENT ⚡: A SPEAKER WE HEARD

We were at a conference recently where a speaker on the stage shared his rags-to-riches story. He talked about how little he had, how he slept in his car because he had no place to stay. Then one day he discovered (insert whatever he discovered), and now he is a changed man. He flashed photos on the screen of his gigantic house overlooking the ocean, his extraordinarily expensive sports car and a lovely, large, loving family.

The speaker was planting seeds of aspiration, surface aspirations but aspirations, nonetheless. The surface aspiration was money. He was appealing to our surface aspiration for more money. In sharing his rags-to-riches story, of course made possible by this amazing program he developed, and then showing you the rewards he received for executing the program steps, he was tapping into the audience's aspiration for more money. So much money your life would be transformed into a state of no worry.

Knowing his audience aspired to make more money he advertised his program as a way to make more money. He peppered his stage presentation with words and pictures of how his program delivered the audience's aspiration for more money. He used the audience's desire for more money as his magnet to attract people to his program.

Yet, money likely wasn't the true and deep aspiration of most of the people in the audience. The question he needed to ask was: why did his Ideal Customer want more money? This question would uncover the deep and true aspirations. Deep and true aspirations bring a power unmatched by a lightning bolt. They dwell deep within, often unspoken. Yet the Ideal Customer craves them and much more than the money, in this example.

Perhaps the attendee to his event wanted to pull their family out of debt or be perceived as a confident and capable breadwinner, or have their confidence lifted, or retire early or create a legacy for their children.

The speaker didn't have an Ah Ha Moment. Instead, he went about his business as usual and garnered the same results as usual…very few people followed him to the back of the room to buy. We offer this Ah Ha Moment that didn't happen, so you can have an Ah Ha Moment of your own without the steep learning curve this guy has.

Surface aspirations scratch at your Ideal Customer's desires. Deep and true aspirations grab the heart. While both expressions of aspirations ring true, which really generates movement? Which one propels a person into action?

Deep and True Aspirations, of course. More money warms our hearts and our bank account. Being able to pull your family out of debt sets the Ideal Customer on fire.

You'll also notice these aspirations have nothing to do with the man on the stage. The aspirations he presented were those of his Ideal Customer, his audience. They weren't about their aspirations to work with the speaker. They were listening to what he said about how he could make their aspiration for a better life come true.

Your Ideal Customer's Aspirations have nothing to do with you, either. Just as in our example, your Ideal Customer wants something for themselves in your area of expertise. They want something for their health, wealth, family, business, elderly parents, kids or maybe themselves.

IF YOU'VE BEEN IN BUSINESS

As with the Built-in Buying Motivators we discussed above, the best way for an established business to identify their Ideal Customer's Aspirations demands listening. You have an opportunity to meet and talk with your Ideal Customer via the phone or in person. Perhaps you've never had this conversation before…a conversation about what moves them. Your time has come. A casual conversation inquiring about what your Ideal Customer aspires to achieve in your area of expertise is a conversation they'll appreciate. People love to talk about their dreams, their desires…their aspirations.

Because you've worked with them already, they have an existing trust in you. They are likely willing to share not just their surface aspirations but also the things deep and true. The more you understand them, the better you will serve them.

Questions you could ask look like these:

- Who besides yourself, are you seeking to help through our work together?

- Before we began working together, what did you aspire to achieve for yourself?

- Why do you want (the aspiration they expressed)?

Listen carefully to their answers as they are providing you with insights into their minds, their motivations, their desires, their aspirations. Invaluable knowledge is about to be handed to you. Invaluable because few businesses possess and even fewer use these insights when speaking with Prospects. Write down what they say, in their language.

TRUST IN YOU
MOVES THEM
TO SHARE
THEIR DEEPEST
ASPIRATIONS.

You might find your Ideal Customer utters generalities. They'll say something like "peace of mind" or "confidence in myself." They utter general answers because no one has ever asked them these questions before. They become tongue-tied. They don't have the words available to express themselves accurately.

The other issue with answers such as those, truth be told, occurs because every single business successfully operating creates peace of mind or confidence for its Ideal Customers. These types of simplifications never hand you the aspirations you seek.

Another question or two must be asked.

How does peace of mind manifest in this area of expertise because peace of mind materializes differently if the area is financial versus wellness? What enables confidence to happen?

Listen carefully to their answer. Your Ideal Customer might need to ponder what you've asked. They don't get asked such meaningful, thought-provoking questions every day. Be patient. Give them time to think about what you've asked and search for the words to accurately express themselves. The words and insights will come.

As you frame your questions, who, what, how and where-type of inquiries produce the best answers. Why questions require inner reflections. Too many why questions cause confusion or murky answers from your Ideal Customer. You'll notice only one "why" question suggested above. This why question is not only permitted but encouraged. The answer to this "why" question will take you to the heart of their aspiration and reveal the reason it's so singularly important to your Ideal Customer.

If it's important to your Ideal Customer, so important they crave it, it should be a critical insight for you to know.

COACHING EXERCISE 7: Identify Your Ideal Customer's Aspirations If You've Been In Business

The questions below are written as though you are your Ideal Customer. They require you to put yourself in the shoes of your Ideal Customer, to answer them as you know or believe your Ideal Customer would answer them. Writing your answers in first person voice (the "I" voice) will bring you closer to the feelings of your Ideal Customer. Give it your very best effort knowing you'll always be able to adjust as you get more experience and more customers.

1. Who besides yourself, are you seeking to help through our work together?

_____

_____

_____

2. When we first began working together, what did you aspire to achieve through our work?

_____

_____

_____

_____

3. Why do you want (the aspiration they expressed)?

_____

_____

_____

_____

4. Now, answering as yourself rather than your Ideal Customer and based on what you've captured from talking with your Ideal Customer, what do you believe are their Surface and Deep/True Aspirations?

_____

_____

_____

_____

IF YOU'RE JUST STARTING YOUR BUSINESS

As a new business owner with few-to-no clients, you'll question your ability to gather these insights into the mind of your Ideal Customer. Without a customer or at least a few available and open to talk, unearthing their aspirations seems impossible. Your Ideal Customer isn't in your presence. If no one has purchased from you, you have yet to build the trust require to ask such personal questions…or so your thoughts tell you. Yet, your Ideal Customer does reside in your presence. Granted, they might not trust you right now with their deepest and most personal thoughts. Yet, you will experience their willingness to share, at a minimum, some of their surface aspirations.

PEOPLE ENJOY TALKING ABOUT THEIR FAVORITE TOPIC… THEMSELVES.

People enjoy talking about themselves. Their favorite topic is themselves (hey, your favorite topic is yourself and ours is us; that's just the way we humans roll). They appreciate someone asking about them, what makes them tick, what they want for themselves. If you honor your relationship with the individual with whom you're speaking…not ask inappropriate questions based on how well and long you've known them…you'll discover most people willingly will honestly answer your questions. As you build your clientele, you'll have the opportunity to develop even deeper insights for a more detailed profile.

Questions you could ask future Ideal Customers could include (general introductory chit-chat questions aside):

- How are you looking to improve your health (or whatever area you operate in)?

- What do you want to achieve for yourself when your health improves (or whatever area you operate in)?

- Who besides yourself, are you seeking to help through taking those steps?

- What do you aspire to achieve?

- Why do you want (the aspiration they expressed)?

At the end of several conversations with prospective Ideal Customers, you'll at least have some fresh insights about their surface aspirations. If you also uncover some of their deeper and true aspirations, you'll done great work! Either way, you're on your way to deeply meaningful insights into the mind of your Ideal Customer.

You'll always have the ability and opportunity to enrich your entire Ideal Customer profile and aspirations as you work in your business. Customers don't stay the same forever. What drove a person to invest in real estate in 2007 isn't the same as today. Aspirations changes drastically and subtlety. If insights you've gathered aren't perfect yet, do not worry. The more frequently you place yourself in the presence of your Ideal Customer the more refined your feel for them will become. And then just as you get settled and confident you know their aspirations, they'll change! That's the fun of working with human beings.

Insights into the mind of your customer requires a constant state of observation. Your Ideal Customer changes and morphs and transforms as their world around them swirls.

. . . .
COACHING EXERCISE 8: *Identify Your Ideal Customer's Aspirations If You're Just Starting Your Business*

The questions below are written as though you are your Ideal Customer. They require you to put yourself in the shoes of your Ideal Customer, to answer them as you believe your Ideal Customer would answer them. Writing your answers in first person voice (the "I" voice) will bring you closer to the feelings of your Ideal Customer. Give it your very best effort knowing you'll always be able to adjust as you get more experience and more customers.

1. What is encouraging you to improve your health (insert your area of expertise rather than health if that doesn't apply to you)?

   _____

   _____

   _____

2. What do you want to achieve for yourself when your health improves (or whatever area you operate in)?

   _____

   _____

   _____

3. Who besides yourself, are you seeking to help through taking those steps?

   _____

   _____

   _____

4. What did you aspire to achieve?

   _____

   _____

   _____

5. Why do you want (the aspiration they expressed)?

_____

_____

_____

YES, THERE WILL BE MULTIPLE AND DIFFERING ANSWERS

Coaches' Question: You might have a lot of answers to all the questions you've asked. In all those answers you're going to find patterns, answers that group around certain insights. Though they might be phrased a bit differently, they lead to the same insight. As you look at what you've gathered, do you see patterns emerging?

When we work with our own Wide Awake Business customers and ask them similar questions to identify the aspirations of their Ideal Customer, we too often hear a random deluge of responses. Our customers begin to tell us what each individual said. They begin to share tens of unique replies.

When you consider each individual customer you have, you will hear multiple and differing answers to your questions. But trying to process hundreds of distinct responses prohibits you from making any useable sense of what you've gathered. When you stop and listen to the answers, you'll discover they begin to form a pattern. You'll have multiple answers, yet when you examine them closely, they will begin to coalesce around only a few aspirations.

FIND THE PATTERNS IN THEIR ANSWERS.

Finding the patterns in your Ideal Customer's aspirations is like how you narrowed down multiple profiles for your Ideal Customer. Usually one or two profiles deliver most of your revenue. Likely a handful of aspirations apply to most of your Ideal Customers.

Let's say you're in the elder care management business. You might have two Ideal Customer profiles as you serve both the elder and their adult children. While we don't encourage you to have more than one Ideal Customer profile, you just might (but no more than two, remember? Resist the urge).

We can use our elder care management owner to show you how to find the patterns in your Ideal Customer's aspirations.

The first question we would ask our elder care business owner: how much of your business comes directly from the elder, they are making the buying decision? Or do the kids inquire and choose the care management company, maybe with input from the parents? In other words, who is the decision maker?

The elder might be paying for the services and may even be consulted about who the kids would like to hire. In this case, the children clearly make the decision and are the Ideal Customer. They are the ones searching to rid their parents…and themselves…of a problem. They are the ones concerned about their elder's health. They are the ones who will do the research to find companies to speak with. They are the ones who will make the calls, check the references and maybe visit the company in person. They are the ones who will choose the care management company. History proves the kids are the decision makers more than 90% of the time. The elder chooses the company to work with only 10% of the time.

Therefore, you must understand the children's aspirations to properly connect with them. As you go digging for the children's aspirations, they will certainly have them for themselves and their elder. You would hear aspirations like:

- I don't want them to fall and hurt themselves

- I want Mom and Dad to be safe

- I want them to live the best life they can under the circumstances

- I need someone else to watch over them as I live too far away to take care of them myself

- I need someone who knows what they are doing as I don't know how to take care of them for what they need right now

These aspirations are Surface and follow two patterns: aspirations for the elder and aspirations for children themselves.

As you get to know the children a little better and as you work with them, you'll begin to hear:

- I don't want to feel like a bad daughter

- I have a family of my own who needs me; I'm torn and overwhelmed by my parents' needs

- Mom frightens me; what if I do something wrong

- I just want to be her daughter again

Now you're getting to the heart, the real deep and true center of their aspirations. Their insights are revealing. The aspirations have become deeply emotional and highly motivating. The child not only fears for their parent, they are scared witless for themselves.

If you were the care management owner, you would search for the patterns in their conversations to find the heart of their aspirations. In this case, the adult child fears for both their parent and certainly themselves. Their fear pushes them to rid both their elder and themselves of the problem. If you were the owner, you'd turn more heads by talking about their fear than only speaking about safety of the elder.

Look for the patterns in your Ideal Customer's Aspirations. Yes, you'll have multiple and differing answers. But a pattern will begin to reveal itself as you look and listen to what they say. One or a couple will stand out beyond all others. The one, singular "why" question we've listed above will draw you to the big, ultimate aspiration. That one "why" question will validate your belief and assumption about what's driving your Ideal Customer.

Remember to overcome general statements of aspirations. Peace of mind, finding their passion and other general statements give you nothing much with which to work. We all provide peace of mind to our Ideal Customers. Otherwise, why be in business? If such statements present themselves when speaking with your Ideal Customers, the next question must be: how does peace of mind manifest when you work with me?

COACHING EXERCISE 9: Find the Patterns in Your Ideal Customer's Aspirations

In the exercises above, you've answered questions as though you were your Ideal Customer. You put yourself in their shoes to be in their brain to recognize their aspirations. In the exercises below, you'll look for the patterns in those answers and turn simplifications into specific aspirations. Give it your very best effort knowing you'll always be able to adjust as you get more experience and more customers.

1. What patterns do you see in the aspirations your Ideal Customer has shared or you believe they have?

_____

_____

_____

2. Sort those patterns into Surface Aspirations and Deep and True Aspirations.

_____

_____

_____

3. If you have broad, general answers (like peace of mind), how does "peace of mind" (or insert your general statement) manifest when your Ideal Customer works with you?

_____

_____

_____

ASPIRATIONS UNITE YOUR IDEAL CUSTOMER PROFILES

ASPIRATIONS UNITE MULTIPLE IDEAL CUSTOMER PROFILES.

Several times we've mentioned...recommended... you identify one Ideal Customer profile. Your small business is likely not big enough to appeal to multiple Ideal Customers. And equally likely, your marketing budget isn't big enough to appeal to multiple Ideal Customers. Remember Seth Godin's truth: small is the new big.

Yet, for some of you, we cannot deny the truth: you do have two Ideal Customer profiles.

While their demographic, psychographic and behaviors might be different, those two Ideal Customer profiles must come together in their Aspirations. If you have two different Ideal Customer profiles and two wildly different Aspirations, you probably have two completely different businesses. More sacrifice, we know. Yet, this sacrifice nets you greater and faster rewards.

The reward for your sacrifice: an easier, simpler and more profitable business.

Let's say you have two Ideal Customer profiles. You want to build your business working with 70-year-old grannies and 18-year-old skateboarders. Hard to find two profiles more unalike! Yet, their aspirations must be the same. In this case, they aspire to a super-duper, high-octane cup of organic, ethically-sourced coffee. They aspire to a jolt and bolt of energy. They aspire to supporting only humane products. They aspire to be a good citizen of the globe.

Now imagine if their aspirations varied. You, as the business owner, would be forced to steady your business to deliver two different things to two different people in a two dissimilar and very crowded, noisy markets. You'd be expecting your Ideal Customer to invest the time to listen very carefully to you and sort through everything you're saying to find the element that speaks to them. You ask them to hang on your every word, sort through two different conversations and find the one meant for them.

They aren't going to do that.

People don't act that way.

Your two Ideal Customers will not take the time from their busy lives to do the work you're supposed to be doing for them. You're required to hand them the message pertinent to them and hand it to them fast.

YOU'RE TO DO THE WORK OF SPEAKING DIRECTLY AND CLEARLY TO YOUR IDEAL CUSTOMER; DON'T ASK THEM TO DO THE WORK; THEY WON'T.

Today's markets whirl, swirl, spit and spin with messages. Your market twirls, too, forcing your Ideal Customer to wade through thousands and thousands of messages every day. Most messages don't connect. Most don't use their language to appeal to them. Most don't repeat a consistent and persistent message long enough for the Ideal Customer to hear it, understand it and whip their head around at full attention. Your Ideal Customer simply cannot devote their time and energy to sorting through your two messages to figure out if they want to hear more or not.

> *Coaches' Question: Think back to the last Facebook link to your content, ad, email campaign...whatever marketing step you've taken most recently. How many times did you run the post with the link? How many ads did you run? How many emails did you send on the promotion? How can you step up your consistency of message to improve your results? You're about to see why.*

Years ago, Martha stumbled on a study commissioned by the National Billboard Association. The study revealed something close to this:

Every day you and I and your Ideal Customer...all of us...are pelted with 2,456 messages. Two thousand four hundred and fifty-six requests to do something. We drive by billboards, get email messages, hear advertising on TV and radio, see ads on Facebook and LinkedIn, get assaulted in elevators by more ads and take a call from your honey to bring home a quart of milk.

Of the 2,456 messages we remember just a small part of 52. Not even the whole message. Just a small part. Perhaps you saw the TV ad last night with the big horses in it. But you have no idea what the product was or the message. You only remember the horses.

Of those 2,456 messages we fully remember 23. The horses were Clydesdales, and Budweiser owned the message.

And here's the real slap-on-the-forehead number. Of those 2,456 messages we only act on 4 every day.

For you to be one of the four acted upon, you must be one of the 23 remembered. One of the 23 remembered not just one day, but on multiple days. You must burst through the market's raging racket. If you're saying one thing to one type of Ideal Customer and something else to another, you will be neither consistent or persistent with your message. Therefore, the odds are terrible you'll be one of the 23 remembered.

These numbers reflect a study Martha unearthed years ago. Don't you believe your markets scream even louder today? That even more messages bomb us daily? That it's harder and harder to be one of the few remembered, not to mention acted upon? Why make it even harder for your Ideal Customer to hear you, turn their heads and look at you through all this noise?

Sacrifice multiple messages for the very few motivating your Ideal Customer. Aspirations motivate. Problems motivate. When you do, you'll be one of a small handful of businesses using insights into the mind of your customers to attract them to you.

• • • • • • • • • • • • • • • • SALES SIDEBAR

Right about now you might be feeling a little overwhelmed about how you'll uncover the right insights into the mind of your Ideal Customer. You've never thought about this critical approach before or had to think from your Ideal Customer's point-of-view rather than yours.

We completely understand. Many of our clients have been overwhelmed, too. That's why we do it for them. It's one of our Team's Super Powers!

COACHING EXERCISE 10:
Check Out What Your Competition Says

This exercise is designed to reveal how unique your message will be when you begin to gather and use insights into the mind of your Ideal Customer. Few of your competitors know the power of insights (unless they, too, bought and read this book!). As proof, this exercise requires you to identify your primary competition (perhaps you lose business to them or they operate in your area), and check out their messages on their website, Facebook page or other ways they communicate to your Ideal Customer.

1. Identify four competitors who do what you do for a living.

_____

_____

_____

2. How are they speaking to their Ideal Customer on their website? What are they telling them?

_____

_____

_____

3. Who are those messages about? The owner of the business? Their services? Or the Ideal Customer?

_____

_____

_____

YOUR IDEAL CUSTOMER PROBLEM

Coaches' Question: Your main goal is to create an easier, simpler and more profitable business, right? To do that you must understand the problem your Ideal Customer is driven to get eliminate completely from their life. Look at how your talking, marketing and selling right now. Are you talking about their problem...or your solution?

You've identified your Ideal Customer profile. You've determined their Buying Motivator. You've thoughtfully unearthed their Aspirations. The last step in gathering insights into the mind of your Ideal Customer detects the problem they have and are actively in motion to solve. This issue keeping them from reaching their Aspirations.

Does your Ideal Customer even have a problem?

If you identified their Buying Motivator above as "away from pain"... and 80% of Ideal Customers are first driven to rid themselves of pain... then your Ideal Customer does have a problem. Maybe they and you call it a challenge or issue instead of a problem. Whatever it's called, your Ideal Customer wants it to go away. They're not just talking a good game yet remain indifferent to its resolution. They really, really, really want this problem out of their life!

Further, if no problem existed, your Ideal Customer would already be experiencing the Aspirations you uncovered. Your Ideal Customer would be moving on to something else. They would have new and different Aspirations.

Using our earlier care management example, the elder would be in a safe place and the child would be feeling more confident they were a good daughter (Surface and Deep/True Aspirations).

But if they are still living with their problem, they haven't achieved their Aspirations. Mom is still not safe, and the daughter is still wringing her hands about being a bad daughter.

Finding the problem your Ideal Customer wants to solve becomes your final task to gain full insights into the mind of your Ideal Customer.

Some problems burst from your Ideal Customer immediately. They will simply tell you. Boom just like that, thank you very much. Be cautious with this information. What they just shared is certainly true. However, that problem might not be their big driver to act.

How do you get to the big driving problem insight if your Ideal Customer shares only the small challenge? How do you get to the real problem when your Ideal Customer won't tell you or you know the real reason and they don't?

DISCOVER YOUR IDEAL CUSTOMER'S BIG PROBLEM TO GAIN THE ULTIMATE INSIGHT.

Two issues yield you from unearthing your Ideal Customer's problem. First, remember you're not a friend to your Ideal Customer. They don't know you very well and trust may not be fully established. They might not know you well enough yet to trust you with the *big* thing on their mind. So they share something that's true and minor. That's still a valuable *insight*. It's just not the most revealing, motivating or activating *problem*. While having the thoughts your Ideal Customer will share with a stranger provides you with something better than nothing, those thoughts probably won't propel your Ideal Customer into action.

Second, you're the expert, not your Ideal Customer. Therefore, you understand the true nature of their problem better than your Ideal Customer does. As the expert, you see the problem in a clearer more accurate light. You know. You see it. You can touch it. You've seen it hundreds of times before.

Your Ideal Customer has no idea.

If you're still stuck scratching your head for your Ideal Customer's problem and how they express it, here are some paths for you to follow.

Interviews: If you have current or former customers, pick up the phone and call them. They've worked with you. The dice roll in your favor when they trust you, and they will share. You can ask them questions like, "When you first said yes to working together, what was the problem you wanted to solve?" Or "What problem brought you to me?" You're going to hear two types of answers. First, you'll hear what we call "will say" answers, answers that are true just not very revealing. Continue with your questions as you can lead them deeper to the "won't say" answers. Won't say answers are deep truths, revealing statements, maybe embarrassing thoughts. Won't say answers will only be uttered to people the Ideal Customer feels they can trust. We'll talk more about "will say," "won't say" and "can't say" answers in just a bit.

Look at Your Reviews: Have people reviewed your business on Yelp, Google or other places? What did they say? You'll find some very honest answers there. Yes, complainers are usually more willing to share than complementors. Yet, insights will be there. If you're not reviewed, are your competitors? What people say about them might reveal bits about the problem they had when they first arrived at your competitor's business.

Use On-line Tools: Using on-line tools puts 21st century technology to work for you. Keyword research enables you to see what people put into the search window to find out more about their problem, who tackles such issues and what possible solutions may be. This isn't the place to teach you how to run a keyword search. You can run a search on how to determine keywords and get the directions to make this work for you.

Ah Ha Moment ⚡: MARTHA AND CHRIS

We have Ah Ha Moments in our own business, too. Our own Wide Awake Business prospects often call us to discuss finally getting on the Facebook bandwagon as a marketing path to get new customers. They believe if they just hop on Facebook, run a couple of ads, make a free offer, people will click the ad and grab the offer. Now they have new people entering their database and can market to them. Our prospect believes their issue revolved around not being fully engaged in social media.

Yet, when we cast our expert eye on their social media presence, or lack thereof, that's not the problem we see. Instead, we see a company that hasn't examined all the steps that come before a social media marketing effort, all the other ducklings that must be in a row. Worse, social media might not even be a very good way to reach their Ideal Customer. Our prospect wanted to hop all over social media because social media developed into the "now" thing to do. Our prospect wasn't using social media. Therefore, they believed they should be doing it. After all, everyone else was doing it!

With our expert eye, we examine their Ideal Customer and often recognize a simple Facebook plan won't move the needle. Likely, their Ideal Customer doesn't even use Facebook to solve the problem they believe they have.

Have we caused you to scratch your head in confusion?

How can you go about gaining insights into your Ideal Customer's problem when:

1. They will only share a surface issue because trust has yet to be built

2. They are too embarrassed to share with a new acquaintance

3. The real problem runs deeper, and they are reluctant to say out it loud to you, a stranger

4. They don't truly know the real problem, and you do

Thankfully, the real heart of your Ideal Customer's problem will be revealed with the process we'll discuss next. Your Ideal Customer's problem spills out in three different ways:

- What they will say

- What they won't say

- What they can't say

WHAT THEY WILL SAY

We agree, right? Your Ideal Customer will share some information about the nature of their problem. While what they articulate might not be their big issue, the problems they share do provide some insights. Gather that information. Capture what they say in their language, not your professional language. Everything they offer contains truth. But know bigger, much more powerful insights hide within your Ideal Customer.

WHAT THEY WON'T SAY

You've got some useful insights with what your Ideal Customer will say to you. Why bother pushing for another level of understandings?

Because there are more important problems your Ideal Customer hasn't shared.

They haven't shared as they are embarrassed or ashamed or afraid to reveal something so personal to someone they don't know very well or respect. Yet, you must know. You must know what they are reluctant to share for here rests the biggest, most motivating insight of all.

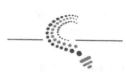

WHAT THEY
WON'T SAY
CONTROLS
THEIR ACTIONS.

Whatever they won't say controls their actions.

The problem they are *unwilling* to express at first...before they don't trust you enough to share and come clean...controls their behavior. Here resides the problem eating at them. The one keeping them up at night. The one pushing them to ask friends, search the Internet or buy something that solves their problem.

What they won't say drives their behavior. But they won't tell you the problem! Sounds like Catch-22. How do you try to uncover this critical piece of information if they won't tell you?

As you turn prospects into Ideal Customers, they will begin to share. Their trust in you builds as they work with you. Their willingness to open up increases. They begin to see you as the source of a solution to their long suffering. What they covered up before they are now willing to offer up. What was so embarrassing earlier in your relationship seems less embarrassing now. What they felt ashamed of feels more calming now. Their fear subsides as they realize you can change their situation.

Listen and ask questions. Their trust in you increased the day they agreed to spend money with you to solve their problem. Their trust grows each day they work with you. Soon they are comfortable and comforted in sharing in the real source of their problem.

Again, that's great news when you've been in business for a time. But how do you gather this must-know if you're just starting out?

You already have an inkling. Remember, you're already an expert. You've got years and years in your field even if you're just starting your business. You most likely have an idea of the real source of the problem from years of working with your Ideal Customer when you worked for someone else. Find a very quiet place to draw out your memories. What did your customers tell you when they got to know you in your j-o-b? What did you glean from those interactions even if they didn't come out and tell you?

YOU HAVE FULL PERMISSION TO SAY WHAT THEY WON'T SAY.

The information rests inside you. It's certainly within your Ideal Customer. Find the problem they won't tell you.

Once you do, you'll use this insight in your business. Your Ideal Customer may be reluctant to utter their real problem out loud, but you can. You can say all the things rolling through your Ideal Customer's head, yet they will not utter it out loud in front of someone new. You can talk about their problem when you're speaking at an event, writing copy for the home page of your website or networking at a meeting.

You have full permission to say what they won't say.

When you do, your Ideal Customer will immediately feel you're talking to them, like you're "inside their head." That's exactly where you want to be, inside their head. As you begin to discuss their problem...the one so personal and perhaps embarrassing they couldn't possibility utter it to you...you have their full, undivided attention.

We do this all the time in our own business. When we're speaking from a stage, we always discuss our Ideal Customer's problem (the ones they won't say), and we talk about it every early in our presentation. As we do, heads nod in agreement. As we come off the stage, people will come up to us and say, "it's like you were inside my head." Truth be told, we were inside their head. That's exactly where we want to be, and where you want to be. In that moment magic happens. The most powerful insight into the mind of your Ideal Customer causes your Ideal Customer to pay attention to you...despite the roar of the market din, in spite of the haze of their indecision and in the face of other possibilities.

Make short work of attracting new prospects. Identify and use the problem they will not say. This powerful insight rules their behavior.

WHAT THEY CAN'T SAY

What they cannot say is the trickiest of the three different ways your Ideal Customer's problem spills out.

What they can't say is the problem you're busy chattering on and on about in your marketing, communications and sales, and your Ideal Customer can't relate to the problem. You're busy talking about a problem or solution they don't understand or never heard of. You're using your expert knowledge to showcase a problem they know nothing about.

STOP TALKING ABOUT WHAT YOUR IDEAL CUSTOMER CANNOT SAY.

As the expert, you fully understand what the true nature of the problem is. Your deep knowledge has enabled you to have x-ray eyes to penetrate down to the source. You've probably seen the real problem a million times before. Your Ideal Customer, on the other hand, has no idea. They've never seen it.

Your Ideal Customer does not see what you see.

The purpose of identifying what your Ideal Customer can't say about their problem is to prevent you from making it the heart of your business, your marketing.

If you persist in talking about a problem your Ideal Customer doesn't believe or recognize they have, your Ideal Customer will not know you exist. You'll be talking, and they will not be hearing.

Can you think of anything worse when gathering up all the Ideal Customer insights we've discussed to this point and then losing your audience because you got technical or super insider-professional on them?

The best way to understand and develop these three ways of finding and expressing your Ideal Customer's problem encourages us to work through an example together.

AH HA MOMENT ⚡: LYDIA

Lydia is a hypnotist, and a Wide Awake Business customer. Her primary Ideal Customers are folks seeking to lose weight or stop smoking. They aspire to weight loss or a smoke-free life as their Surface Aspiration. Their Deep/True Aspirations run deeper. They don't want to be embarrassed by how they look not only to others, but more importantly, themselves. Perhaps they've tried other methods...many methods...to lose the weight or stop smoking. In each case they've failed in the long-run. They are frustrated and don't know where to turn to reach their Aspirations.

Lydia's Ideal Customers' Problems:

Will Say:

- I want to lose weight I can't seem to take off

- I am tired of not being able to beat my cigarette habit

- I want to live a long and healthy life

What They Won't Say:

- I want to stop being embarrassed by my appearance

- I hate the fact I smell like smoke

- My kids keep asking me to lose the weight or to stop smoking, and I want them to be proud of me

What They Can't Say:

- Hypnotism can cure weight gain and a smoking habit

- Mastering my subconscious will end my weight or smoking issue

Lydia now has a foundation of insights into the mind of her Ideal Customer. She wants to use them in her business to attract new prospects. She could say:

"I solve your weight loss problems...forever!"

Or she could lead with:

"You no longer have to be embarrassed by how your weight makes you feel."

Or she could say:

"Mastering your subconscious will eliminate your weight problem."

If you had a weight challenge, which message would grab your attention?

Certainly, you could relate to "I solve your weight loss problems...forever." You've probably heard it a hundred times from other weight loss experts. The problem is real. The statement is true. It addresses Lydia's Ideal Customer's problem. It's just not super original. A good approach, not great.

"You no longer have to be embarrassed by how your weight makes you feel." This statement, unlike the one above, is deeply emotional. It lands smack on the real, profound, unspoken problem her Ideal Customer feels about carrying extra weight. Her Ideal Customer feels embarrassed, maybe ashamed. This insight speaks to the unspeakable. It grabs attention in its originality and truthfulness. Lydia's Ideal Customer will feel Lydia's in their head.

If Lydia used "mastering your subconscious will eliminate your weight problem," she most likely would have an uphill struggle to get her Ideal Customer to view her message. The odds of them looking to master of their subconscious as the solution to their problem is highly unlikely. Most won't even know their subconscious affects their overeating. If Lydia changed her message to talk about hypnosis as the route to weight loss, her Ideal Customer may not pay attention either. Many people fear or are put off by hypnosis.

Lydia followed our insight-driven recommendation. She began to eliminate her "can't say" talk that had dominated her conversations, website and email campaigns. We wrote out her new way to introduce herself using the "won't say" problems Lydia had gleaned from her years in business. More heads began to nod "yes." We gave her input on changes to her email campaigns to produce better results and adjusted her phone conversations. It took Lydia a bit of time to change her approach. What she had been doing was so ingrained. With time she became comfortable with the transformation in how she presented herself to her Ideal Customer. Her business became much simpler.

Now, which of the three messages would you use if you were Lydia?

Precisely. The insights they won't say.

The same rings true for your Ideal Customer. And that's exactly what Lydia did!

COACHING EXERCISE 11: *Your Ideal Customer's Problem*

This exercise is designed to reveal how unique your message will be when you begin to gather and use insights into the mind of your Ideal Customer. Few of your competitors know the power of insights (unless they too bought and read this book!).

1. What do you believe is your Ideal Customer's problem? Your opinion?

_____

_____

_____

_____

2. Now, change your position and think like your Ideal Customer. What is the problem your Ideal Customer believes they have and will say? Use the words your Ideal Customer uses.

_____

_____

_____

_____

3. What is the problem your Ideal Customer believes they have and won't say? Using the words your Ideal Customer uses.

_____

_____

_____

_____

4. What is the problem your Ideal Customer cannot say? They don't realize the real source of their issue or the solution is unfamiliar to them. Of course, since you're Ideal Customer doesn't know about this problem, you cannot use their words. Now you're using your words.

_____

_____

_____

_____

5. When you use search tools to gain insight into the kinds of problems (and words) your Ideal Customer uses to search for that problem, what words and phrases did you discover?

_____

_____

_____

_____

> Remember, all these Coaching Exercises are available
> to you, along with special offers on our website:
> wideawakebusiness.com/resources

BRING YOUR INSIGHTS TOGETHER

Your Ideal Customer profile *coupled* with a firm understanding of their built-in buying motivator *plus* an accurate articulation of their aspirations, both surface and deep/true *and* a public discussion of the problem they want to solve yet won't say out loud...

WHAT CAN YOU DO FOR YOUR IDEAL CUSTOMER?

...my goodness, the influence you now have.

Insights into the mind of your Ideal Customer transform your business.

First, your Ideal Customer can hear you. You'll be speaking directly to them in a language they can receive about the thing most important to them.

Next, remember to check out your competition. Are they using insights into the mind of their Ideal

Customer, the same customer you want to attract? We're betting not. It's always stunning to us how few businesses...gigantic, large and small... are busy talking about themselves and have no idea how to speak to their customers using what motivates them into action.

Your Ideal Customer's interest in you stems solely from what you can do for them. Why would you waste a moment chattering about yourself at the beginning of the relationship?

They don't care about you.

They don't care about your product or service.

They care about themselves, about their aspirations in life, about batting down the hurdles keeping them from attaining their aspiration, about removing the problem they actively want to solve. Something as small as working to unearth these insights can transform your business from one where you struggle to one that's easier, simpler and much more profitable.

Take the high road or the wrong road. The choice is yours.

PURSUING YOUR IDEAL CUSTOMER

Even though you've narrowed your Ideal Customer profile to a small, easily identifiable space, not every person meeting that definition will be your Very Best Ideal Customer.

In an irreverent, but not religious, sort of way we think about potential customers in three ways: as Believers, Atheists and Agnostics.

Believers understand what you're talking about almost as soon as you start speaking about their Aspirations and Obstacles. They smack their foreheads and wonder where you've been all their life. They recognize quickly you're the answer to the problem they've been seeking to solve. You say it; they get it. Rapid engagement.

IS YOUR PROSPECT A BELIEVER, ATHEIST OR AGNOSTIC?

Then there are the Atheists. They, too, hear you and understand rapidly. They completely "get" what you're saying. Yet, they argue. They bat around other ideas, challenge your assumptions and generally give you a taxing time. They feel like a Believer...they comprehend what you're saying. You feel if you keep talking...just adjust something a little bit...they'll turn into a Believer. They won't. You want to recognize the difference between your Believers and Atheists and do it quickly as Atheists can suck all your time and attention in the belief they are your people. Atheists waste your time. Move on as soon as you recognize them for what they are.

Agnostics do not know what you're talking about. They have no knowledge of what you speak. Agnostics present a different issue. They elongate your sales cycle because you must, first, education them on the problem and the fact you are skilled at eliminating that problem. As you speak to them again and again (50 times?), they become more knowledgeable. They will then need to determine if they believe and agree with you. If so, they turn into a Believer. If they don't, you have an Atheist in your midst. You're sure to encounter some Agnostics in your business.

But if your message is clear…and based firmly on your Ideal Customer's Aspirations and Obstacles, spoken in their language…you'll likely have a great prospect. If your message isn't clear, you'll discover the path to a "YES" will grow long.

> *Coaches' Question: Yes, this is an unusual way to think about your prospects. And also highly memorable. Thinking this way will speed the time you spend with each prospect and enable you to understand to whom to make your offer, walk away or tell them more. What clues will you look for to enable you to spot your Believers, Atheists and Agnostics?*

PART THREE

Act Like Your Customer

Coaches' Question: When you set out to develop and implement a new approach...which is what you're about to do in this section of Customertopia...ask yourself "what must I shed to adopt something new, better and more effective to reach my overarching goal? What is not serving me well?" You're making room for a critical transformation in you and your business.

YOUR HUMAN CONVERSATION

Grab a pot and fill it with water. Put it on the stove and crank up the heat until the water reaches 200 degrees. Wait and watch. The water warms, but nothing much changes. Now push the heat up to 211 degrees. Wait and watch. Can you see a change? Nope. Now add one more tiny little degree. Just one more itty bitty degree of warmth! The water in your pot roils to a boil!

What you're about to do with all the spot-on Ideal Customer insights you've gathered will turn your business into a steaming, roiling pot of hot, boiling goodness because you're turning up the warmth just a few degrees.

The catalyst thrusting you from tepid water to crazy boil requires you to take those insights you've created in **Part 2, Think Like Your Customer,** and do something with them. That's what you're going to do in **Part Three, Act Like Your Customer**. Do something. Not just anything. The very right thing to build a bridge from you to your Ideal Customer (not from them to you, if you see the difference).

BUSINESS IS FUNDAMENTALLY HUMAN.

To build a strong, firm bridge to your Ideal Customers you must recognize…

…*business is fundamentally human.*

Everything else comes in a distant second.

Business is human. Human conversation…genuine, authentic, empathic, insightful conversation… drives the language and actions of successful companies. Your finest business occurs when you, the person on the inside of your business, have the fullest contact with your Ideal Customers on the outside. You can't hide behind your website or email campaigns. You can't operate out of your office or home without heading out. You can't expect to connect with Ideal Customers without picking up the phone to call or visiting them at events, meetings or their office.

You know how to be human, but perhaps you've forgotten. In this age of everything amped up by the Internet, people want you to believe it's the force behind success.

Yet, humans still relate to humans. Technology remains second-rate.

If you have formal business training garnered in the 70s, 80s and even 90s, most of what they taught, and you learned, can be tossed. You'll reshape that formal business education with smarts from the street…where

YOUR HUMAN CONVERSATION BUILDS YOUR BRIDGE TO YOUR IDEAL CUSTOMER.

your humans walk, talk and live. Those smarts come from having and using insights into the mind of your Ideal Customer.

The conversations (okay, we can also call it marketing and sales because that's what it is; those aren't evil words) you construct using insights into the mind of your Ideal Customers will create melodies playing in their heads. Some melodies hit serious notes, maybe even sad as you talk about Aspirations not yet met and Problems not yet solved. Some songs will be filled with laughter at the silliness of the Problem. Still a few others will ring with tones of the joy and happiness from a vitamin downed for their betterment.

Every melody will be built on a human conversation. Every conversation will be constructed on your Ideal Customer insights.

Your human conversation builds your bridge to your Ideal Customer.

Your conversation forms the foundation of your business. If you've lost your human voice because of corporate-speak or an inability to perfectly articulate the problem...or perhaps you never had it (didn't know you needed it due to that errant education from years ago), you're about to regain it.

The most successful small businesses speak the language of their Ideal Customer and utter it from the heart.

HUMAN CONVERSATION CREATES YOUR CUSTOMER PLATFORM

Your powerful, new conversation (hello, marketing and sales ingredients) feels open, honest, direct, empathetic, funny and sometimes shocking. The conversation centers on your Ideal Customer, showcasing your complete understanding of their problem and ability to rid them of it. You're tossing away the monotone of a mission statement (your Ideal Customer doesn't care; your employees might). You're pitching the platitudes in your brochures and website. You're throwing away your ineffective Call-to-Action, because it didn't call anyone anywhere.

You'll replace all of that with your human voice, reflecting their human desires.

Coaches' Question: To get into the spirit of being human again...to support your transformation to a customer-centered business...create your Customer Platform, your personal declaration of your desire to transform how your Ideal Customers see, hear and connect with you. Your Customer Platform could include statements like:

1. My customer has a problem; I understand their problem and have exceptional expertise in eliminating it

2. We talk to my Ideal Customer in sincere, genuine, authentic human language, mimicking their sincere, genuine, authentic human language

3. *My responsibility is to build my business from my Ideal Customer's perspective, not mine*

4. *In building my business from my Ideal Customer's perspective...with them in the center of everything I do...I'm moving my ego aside. It's not about me, my products or services. It's about my customer.*

5. *I understand it's my responsibility to eliminate the two conversations going on, one within my business and one within my Ideal Customer. Only my Ideal Customer's conversation matters.*

6. *As a customer-centered business, I realize it's my responsibility to construct a customer-centered bridge from me out to my Ideal Customer*

These are merely six starter thoughts for your own Customer Platform. What will you create to enable your customer resolve to strengthen and be showcased to your Ideal Customer? We're not suggesting you post your "Customer Platform" somewhere. Rather, this is an exercise for you to begin to step into acting like your Ideal Customer because you've flipped your business to be centered on them. Build it with your Team as they will be a part of making the Platform real or just words.

THE TRANSFORMATION OF YOU

You've been you for a very long time. From the beginning, as a matter of fact.

Now you're going to channel someone else.

You're going to become your Ideal Customer. Not perfectly because you're still the expert they are not. You remain the professional who can solve their problem. In your initial steps to find a person, build them to become an Ideal Prospect and work with the Ideal Prospect to turn into your Ideal Customer, you're going spend a lot of time in the head of your Ideal Customer rather than yours.

Let us show you what a transformation looks like, so you have an idea of where you're headed using our client, Lydia, who you met earlier.

AH HA MOMENT ⚡: LYDIA

Recently, Lydia sent us an email she wanted to send to her database of smokers. The email draft looked like this (we're taking out some of the contact me information to protect Lydia from a barrage of emails).

Hi (insert name),

Who do you know that is struggling to put down those unhealthy cigarettes, and shout with pride, "I AM A NON-SMOKER!"?

I can show them how.

I am proud to tell you that I have been a Certified Hypnotist for 26 years, and I have helped a lot of people quit smoking using my proven Stop Smoking NOW! System. I know what works, and I know what doesn't work.

I know what it feels like to see someone you love suffering, because my Dad died from smoking. He developed throat and lung cancer and lived only three months after his diagnosis. He is one of the reasons that I became a hypnotist. I remember thinking to myself after I was certified, "I sure wish Dad had met a hypnotist, then maybe, just maybe he would have lived a lot longer."

I help people all over the world stop smoking using hypnosis by phone and/or online with the Zoom app.

Your life, or your loved-one's life as a non-smoker starts here.

Lydia did okay with this email. Yet, she wanted to do better. Read this email a second time. We'll wait right here for you.

Who is this email about? Lydia or her Ideal Prospect? Count the number of "I" words appearing in the message. Her messages focused more on Lydia than her Ideal Prospect. This email (thank you, Lydia, for permitting us to use it) offers a good example of thinking and acting from your own perspective...creating a conversation about you.

Instead, Lydia's email could look like this...speaking the language of her humans.

Hi xx,

You've told yourself you're going to "let go" of your smoking habit. You mean it. It's the easiest advice to give yourself...and the hardest to follow.

Then the challenging moment arrives. "I'm not smoking the next cigarette," you say. But the urge overwhelms you. "Let it go. It's okay. I won't have the next one." Yet, the next one and the next one call to you despite your determination to let go of smoking.

You can quit smoking by December 31…*this year.*

You might believe that sounds too good to be true. You've tried so many ways to stop smoking.

You haven't tried my way, proven over 26 years.

My quit-smoking methodology has enabled thousands of people to toss their cigarettes away…for good. Want proof? Take a look at the photo in this email. My clients pitch their last pack of cigarettes into a jar when they've mastered a smoke-free life. I've emptied that jar a hundred times!

Isn't it worth a simple, no-obligation exploratory conversation to investigate if this quit-smoking methodology would be right for you?

You can choose a time that works best for you simply by clicking the link below and scheduling a conversation. (click to her on-line schedule)

Your life as a non-smoker starts with a click. You really can quit by December 31st!

The difference between the two emails clearly illustrates what it looks and feels like to convert from your language to the language (problem) of your humans (Ideal Customer). The second email uses the word "you" far more than "I." "You" is your Ideal Customer's favorite word. "I" shut down their eyes, ears and interest. The second email uses the words Lydia's Ideal Customer uses when they first speak with her about their great desire to stub out the butts.

And in an advanced lesson, the second email also pops a likely and interest-killing thought going through their mind as they read the email: this is too good to be true. Before Lydia's Ideal Customer can even think "this is too good to be true," Lydia tackles it, recognizing their disbelief and eliminating it with the truth.

• • • • • • • • • • • • • • • • • • • **SALES SIDEBAR**

We did write this second email for Lydia. Our copywriters stand at the ready to do the same for you, to aid you in your transformation (yes, another example we're more than just a pretty face!) This is us asking for your business. Are you asking for the business in your books?

The Transformation of You begins by putting down your expert knowledge and picking up your Ideal Customer's problem, as you see in the Lydia email above. In the process of connecting to your Ideal Customer, creating an honest conversation about the problem they believe they have is Step 1.

Step 2 injects you into the transformation.

YOU AND YOUR IDEAL CUSTOMER

Most of the conversation you'll create (in your marketing and sales) comes from your Ideal Customer's problem. Yet, there must be a place for you, too. Otherwise, your Ideal Customer will understand you understand them, but they won't have much of a handle on you.

Once you've turned your Ideal Customer's head by sharing a great conversation about them and their problem and pulling them to you because you're inside their head talking about the things they "won't say," they become curious about you.

Your Ideal Customer interest in you peeks. Who is this person who "gets" me, who understands what I'm going through and has empathy for my situation? They become curious enough to take a peek at you, what you do that makes you so special and able to tackle their problem. People call this step by many names. We're not sure there's one we love.

- Branding: there's more to branding than just words; there's graphics and logos and many other things

- Unique Selling Proposition (USP): we like the "unique" part; but as soon as you start thinking about how you sell, you're turned back in towards you rather than building from your Ideal Customer's position

- Positioning: we use this expression most of the time; again, it's not our favorite because it's marketing lingo, rather than plain Ideal Customer speak

So we're settled on calling it your Hook.

Your Hook holds the information your Ideal Customer wants to know once you've caught their attention through speaking their language, using the insights you've gleaned.

Your Hook contains two important pieces of information about you:

1. The field within which you operate
2. What makes you so special

IDENTIFYING YOUR FIELD

Holy Moses. If identifying the field in which you operate isn't one of the easiest things you do with us, we're at a loss for what will be!

You know you're an accountant, CPA, financial planner, care manager, insurance broker, massage therapist, dog walker, tutor, business consultant, chocolate maker, tutor, educational coach or whatever you do. So far in the public conversation you've had with your Ideal Customer, they don't know that. They know you understand their problem, and you have plenty of experience in making it go away. What they don't know is "how" you make it go away. What's your expertise? You now have their attention, and they are curious about you.

That said, there are many ways your Ideal Customer could follow to have their problem evaporate. Ideally, you've attracted them to you before they searched for one of the many paths open to them.

Lydia can solve the problem of how to quit smoking. Lots of other disciplines can solve the problem, too. Hypnotism isn't the only path. Search for "how to quit smoking," and you'll discover patches, pills, coaches, advice sites, essential oils, devices, vitamins and a host of other approaches.

Once Lydia's Ideal Customer is attracted to her message…because it's their problem…they want to know how she does it. They've probably tried the patches, pills, advice sites, oils or some crazy approach (eating cigarettes…really) without success. Why take the same approach again? They believe they will only experience the same results. Lydia's approach is hypnotism. While that might spook some of her Ideal Customers, others who have tried everything will be open to the idea.

At some point Lydia will share that's her field, her successful approach to putting an end to smoking. While it's usual information, it doesn't make her special or separate her from other hypnotists working with smokers.

You too operate successfully in some field of endeavor. You're a doctor, dentist, chiropractor, coach, care manager, financial planner, hypnotist, real estate agent, CPA, bookkeeper, software developer, elder care provider, residential contractor, architect, lead generator, sales specialist, property manager, court reporter...you get it.

What's your area of specialty in your field? Let's say you're a coach. And you're a good coach. You can coach almost anything. You might even be able to narrow it down to business coaching. You can coach business people, managers in some sort of transition, couples who also work together in their business, executives who want to advance their careers, teams aiming for higher performance, owners seeking a succession plan, sons and daughters trying to get Dad to step aside, women wanting to sell their business. Have we forgotten any? Probably.

You don't have the time, money or ability to grab the attention of your Ideal Customer when you share you do every type of coaching. That sucks you back into "anybody who..." and "everybody who..." You know there's no value there.

YOU CAN'T BOIL THE OCEAN.

You can't be everything to everybody. Attempting to do everything (even if you really can do everything) would be likened to an attempt on your part to boil the ocean. Good luck with that! Boiling the ocean means you're trying to undertake a task, project, business that's impossible to achieve.

WHAT PROBLEM DO YOU WANT

Yes, it's completely possible you could solve every problem all those people in need of a coach face. You could. You have the talent. Here's the thing...your Ideal Customer doesn't have the patience or time to sift through everything you're saying and not saying to determine if you are meant for them.

A great Hook creates your bridge to your Ideal Customer. Your Hook showcases the thing that makes you valuable, special and so worth checking out. A broad Hook makes it very difficult for your Ideal Customer to understand and engage. Instead of you being all over the place (likely because you are

WHAT PROBLEM DO YOU WANT.

again worried about not attracting all the business you can get), a narrowly-focused Hook bursts through the sludge.

Remember...your Ideal Customer is pelted every day with thousands of requests for their attention. When your Hook is straight-forward, spot-on, you can machete your way through the noise.

The question that enables you to refine your Hook?

What problem do you want?

AH HA MOMENT ⚡ : KAREN

Karen is the CEO of a very successful care management practice. Her Ideal Customers are elders and their family members seeking a guidance to care for themselves or their loved one as they age, and capabilities become more daunting. Most of the time, her Ideal Customers come to her either during a health crisis or shortly thereafter. Mom falls and hurts herself or Dad's driving skills have deteriorated as evidenced by his recent fender bender. Karen's business is good, and she clearly knows her business provides an aspirin as her Ideal Customers come to her when problems arrive. Her Ideal Customer doesn't have a background in senior health options, nor do they have any experience navigating the increasingly complex medical maze.

Karen's thrilled with the work her business does, yet it's focused on the negative...what elders can no longer do competently or safely. Karen yearns to focus on wellness, to work with the same Ideal Customer proactively...before a serious issue arises. Yet, as you know from our earlier work here in Customertopia, the vast majority of Ideal Customers are pushed into action by a problem, not to make something pretty good wonderful.

Karen's quandary: what problem does she want? Does she want the problem of tackling the health problems of elders and their families, or does she want to evolve into a wellness company with the goal of keeping seniors in the best health possible before a problem arises?

If Karen chooses to continue to be a care management company, it appears she gives up her great desire to have her business tackle elder wellness. If she chooses to be a wellness company, the size of her market shrivels substantially.

What problem does Karen want?

We coached Karen to the realization she can have both. We're not advising Karen she can have it all, "anyone who" or "everyone who." Karen's company can continue to be a care management company working to make difficult senior health issues more manageable, to lead in the market with the problem as they have always done. To move more towards her heart's desire, Karen will add wellness services available to her seniors *when their health issues have moved out of crisis stage.*

Karen is adjusting the services she offers, not the Hook of the company she promotes.

Karen's Ah-Ha moment enabled her to have the company she wanted, without adjusting how the local marketplace knows her business. She will add the wellness services near to her heart. The problem Karen wanted…to be a wellness company…is possible by adding services, not by changing the company's approach to the market.

AH HA MOMENT ⚡: KELSEY

Kelsey runs a very successful lead generation business. Her Ideal Customers say they want more leads but aren't experts in that field. They have tried without much success to attract new customers. Kelsey has a system that attracts leads that match the profile her Ideal Customer desires. The challenge for Kelsey isn't in her system's ability to attract leads. She's proven her company can do that. Kelsey hands the new prospects to her Ideal Customer for them to take it from there, to have conversations with the prospects and sell them, turn them into their Ideal Customer. Well, many of Kelsey's Ideal Customers don't have enough sales acumen to close the sale. They aren't skilled at turning a good lead into a prospect into an Ideal Customer. If Kelsey's Ideal Customers don't have the skill to turn a lead into a customer then her Ideal Customer believes the program wasn't a success. Yes, the Ideal Customer asked for leads. They got leads. What they really wanted was a customer.

Kelsey must sort through what problem she wants. Does she want to be the lead generation company and hand the sales skill training to an affiliate company? If she does that, her Ideal Customer will likely take money from Kelsey's lead generation program and hand it to the sales training company. Then Kelsey's company reduces its revenue. If Kelsey decides she wants the problem of training her Ideal Customers on sales, she'll need to hire additional team, yet likely generate less revenue. Her Ideal Customers will be happy because they'll have more customers. But Kelsey will incur additional expense without the additional reward of more revenue.

Kelsey's quandary is difficult. It feels like a "got cha" at every turn. Yet, if she doesn't choose the problem she wants, her business will have a difficult time growing easily, simply and more profitably. As of the time Customertopia has gone to press, Kelsey is still sorting through with our help to choose her problem.

In deciding what problem you want, you're making a choice, agreeing to the trade-offs. You're deliberately choosing to be something special rather than everything in general. Now you're getting closer to your Hook. More sacrifice, yes. More reward? Definitely.

COACHING EXERCISE 12: *The Problem You Want*

1. You are an expert. You can solve a ton of customer problems. List all the problems you solve below.

_____

_____

_____

_____

_____

2. Of all those problems you listed above, what is the central—main—problem you solve? And does your Ideal Customer want that problem solved? Refer back to your *Coaching Exercises* in Part Two: Think Like Your Customer. Has your thinking advanced as you've read and worked here? Or have you reverted to your old you-centered way of thinking?

_____

_____

_____

_____

_____

YOUR BRIDGE TO YOUR IDEAL CUSTOMER

Choosing the problem you want will propel you to build the bridge from you to your Ideal Customer. The bridge represents how you travel from you towards them and how you present yourself to your Ideal Customer when you see them. For your Ideal Customers to look at you, see you, be attracted to you in this noisy world, you must be saying something incredibly relevant to them.

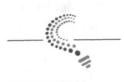

YOUR IDEAL CUSTOMER'S FAVORITE TOPIC IS THEM.

And what could be more relevant than talking about them…their favorite subject!

Think of your bridge as your Hook.

Your Hook secures your Ideal Customer to you. Your Hook blasts through the market nonsense because you are saying something valuable to your Ideal Customer. Your Hook clearly demonstrates you "get" your Ideal Customer's problem.

Your Hook does one other critical thing: it showcases your Super Power, your unique and unassailable ability to eliminate your Ideal Customer's problem.

In our book, *Customers Are the Answer to Everything*, we define Your Hook and the process to enable you to uncover it. The process remains as strong today as it was when we first published. It's well worth revisiting here. We wrote it based on a process Martha and Wide Awake Business have used for decades, and we're happy to report it stands the test of this new market as well.

READY, SET, DIFFERENTIATE

Your Hook showcases how you are different from everybody else out there who does what you do. Think of it as your Super Power. You're able to leap over building in a single bound. Only Superman can do that. You're able to fight off enemy fire with your Bracelets of Submission. Only Wonder Woman has that power. Figuring out how you are different requires you to see yourself not only as you are, but also as others see you. Get outside yourself and take a good look.

We've got a process to enable you to do that. The process starts with a little free-form rambling, a brainstorm. All ideas are good ideas during a brainstorm. No editing or critiquing or belittling yourself during your brainstorm.

Let's start by looking at what you'll be brainstorming. While brainstorming, let go of all your current ideas about what makes you different. Remember: no self-editing at this stage.

Remember, all these Coaching Exercises are available to you, along with special offers on our website: wideawakebusiness.com/resources

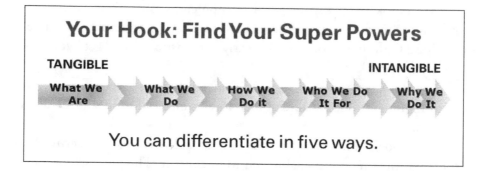

The left-hand side of the worksheet represents very "Tangible" ways you are different. As you move farther to the right, your ideas will become more "Intangible." That means the items you list on the left are the most real, touchable. As you move all the way to the right, things become less concrete, and also more unique to you. And the farther to the right your go, the harder it is for the competition to follow you, as you'll see.

The first column, **"What We Are,"** is a highly factual description of who you are. It's more than just a description of the category you work in, such as coach, insurance broker, dentist and so on. Please think about how to describe yourself a bit differently than others in your field. For example, you are a Type A Coach, or The Listening Doctor, or The First Time

Seller's Realtor. While this column is very practical, it's the perfect place to position yourself if you are doing something no one has done before. When Yahoo launched the first Internet information portal, they found their Hook here in What We Are.

The second column, **"What We Do,"** captures the services or products you provide and the benefits your Ideal Prospect receives from working with you. If you were a coach, you might list things like "I coach people through divorce. I relieve the stress that ties you in knots from divorce." You'll have lots of brainstorm entries in this column. If you make a unique product or provide a special service, this is an ideal place to find your positioning.

The third column, **"How We Do It,"** captures a process or the "way" you provide the product or service. For example, "We use only sustainable manufacturing processes," or "We have created a proprietary, experiential learning process." This is a particularly good place for those of you in a service business to find your differentiation because you might have a very unique methodology when delivering your service.

The fourth column, **"Who We Do It For,"** is about your Ideal Customer. This is where you capture information about "who" your customer is. For example, "We create financial services for young families with children under the age of 6." We love to find what makes you different in this column, and not enough companies use it. Your customers might have very unique profiles or needs. If they do and you know them, you can build you're your Hook on their uniqueness. In other words, their uniqueness becomes yours.

The fifth column, **"Why We Do It,"** really speaks to your passion, your vision, what compels you, what's in your heart, what likely sparked your desire to go into business. What makes this such a rich place to differentiate yourself, to find your Hook, rests in the fact this is *your* passion—not your competitors'. Consumer-oriented companies seem more willing to create their Hook on their passion than left-brained, business-to-business companies. That doesn't mean if you're a left-brained business you should avoid talking about your passion. Quite the contrary. We encourage you to spend some time on this column as it provides such extraordinary opportunities to separate yourself. We love Disney as an example. They differentiate themselves on their passion—*they put magic in your life*. Everything from their theme parks to their short-lived breakfast cereal to Disney cruises positions around putting magic in your life. Disney competes with Universal, but Universal doesn't tell you they put magic in your life. Immediate separation for Disney. And now you know why your kids tug at your sleeves to go there!

Once you start brainstorming, what might your ideas look like? Here are the ideas that came up for Vetrazzo, a company creating stunningly beautiful surfaces and counter tops made from recycled glass.

WHAT WE ARE:

- Unique, visual solid surface using recycled glass
- Art from recycled glass
- The first distinctive, artful solid surface using recycled glass
- Best choice for self-expression

WHAT WE DO

- Create stunning, bold, lively playful mixes
- Using 90% recycled materials
- Enable unique, personal expression of style and values in solid surface building materials
- Style that respects earth and environment
- Combine gorgeous and good into a single style
- Create solid-surface art work for homes and buildings
- Let your home or building tell story of who you are
- Put a story in every surface (because the recycled glass often comes from interesting sources)

HOW WE DO IT

- Mixing bold, lively, dynamic pieces of recycled glass
- Patents
- Building to and beyond the standards of granite

- Recognizing that art/beauty live in unique uses for reclaimed glass
- Recognizing that recycling affects local and global change

WHO WE DO IT FOR

- People who want to make a statement in their homes, buildings and world
- People who want to leave their signatures on their homes, buildings and world
- People who want to express their unique values
- People who don't want their kitchen and projects to look like everyone else's project

WHY WE DO IT

- Gorgeous and good
- Make a statement about you
- It's beautiful to do the right thing
- Sustainable WOW
- Nothing expresses your values like gorgeous and green

COACHING EXERCISE 13: *Search For Your Hook Through Differentiation*

This is a brainstorming exercise. Don't hold back. Write down everything you know or believe to be true about you and your business.

1. What You Are:

_____

_____

_____

2. What You Do:

_____

_____

_____

_____

3. How You Do It:

_____

_____

_____

_____

4. Who You Do It For:

_____

_____

_____

_____

5. Why You Do It:

_____

_____

_____

_____

THE TAKE-AWAY

It's time to face some truth—most of your Ideal Prospects are not even shopping for what you "make," and we use that word whether you make chocolate candies or your make consulting services. They most likely have no idea they should be investigating what you do. Statistics show only 3 to 5 percent of your Ideal Prospects are out shopping for what you make. What are the rest of your Ideal Prospects doing? They are looking for ways to take away their headaches or make their life better. They just don't know you take away their headache or make their life better. It's your job to show them.

Therefore, the benefit your Ideal Prospect seeks is the specific relief they feel when you take that big, old headache away or you enable them to make their life better, as they've been trying and failing to do on their own.

Always remember the kicker: people spend their money, first, on things that take away their headaches. If they have any money left over, then they do something nice for themselves. Therefore, you want your business to be the aspirin that takes away their headache, not the vitamin that makes something better.

CRAFT YOUR HOOK STATEMENT

The next step in the Positioning process creates the really big excitement. You're going to determine which ideas on your Differentiation Worksheet are the Super Power-iest. You're sifting for those Powers that not only showcase your specialness, they also align with what's important to your Ideal Customer. Which point an arrow towards the most important, most unique, most differentiating? Sift for no more than four Super Powers that really emphasize the essence of you.

You've narrowed down your Super Powers to no more than four, right?

Perfect. Now look at those four—which one has the most power, the Supreme Super Power of Super Powers? Which one can you build your company on? Which one separates you the best from your competition? Which ones shines the bright light on what your Ideal Customer desires? Take that one attribute and make it your Super Power.

You have the centerpiece of your Hook, your Super Power. Next you'll mix in "ingredients" for what we call your "Elevated Ingredients." It's not your Elevator Speech, rather you'll doodle all the ingredients you need to craft your Elevator Introduction, presentation intro, banners, flyers, maybe your personal bio and other marketing and sales tools. You can use the ingredients as the foundation for the About Us copy on your website. While you will never recite all of the ingredients word-for-word, your Elevated Ingredients provide you with the ingredients to build the language and communications bridge to your Ideal Customer.

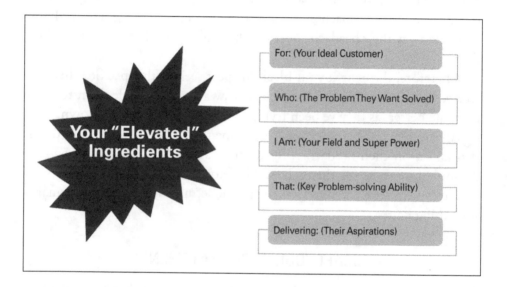

Your Elevated Ingredients will create a short-and-straight-to-the-point statement about your business. Resist the urge to talk and talk in your desire to share everything before the prospect moves on to something… or someone…else. All you want to do right now is share something *compelling* enough to prompt further inquiry, a comment like "Wow, that's so interesting. Tell me more about that." Engage someone's interest. Communicate what's unique and different about you. Claim their mind for at least a little bit. If they become more curious, they are handing you the opportunity to elaborate. This is your moment! Talk more about the problems you solve for people, the benefits they receive from working with you, and then "close" them on a next step or "Call To Action."

Watch your use of "I," "We," "Us," "Our," "Me" or "My." They derail the conversation from the Ideal Customer's point-of-view to yours. And, of course, don't use jargon. Think of how many times you have asked someone the question, "What do you do," and you've heard a long ramble with ideas or concepts that make no sense to you. You probably felt bored or even alienated and made the fastest excuse you could think of to move away from this person.

Here are some Elevated Ingredients showcasing a great Hook, built on the company's Supreme Super Power of Super Powers:

- "For women who want a primary physician with a natural approach to menopause and women's health concerns, Dr. K. is "The Listening Doctor" who gets to the root cause of your problems."

- "Reverend J works with seekers on a spiritual path who struggle to live their beliefs in their daily lives, showing them how to "walk their talk," heal and find the way into the true place of joy."

- Engine 5 works with medical device companies, both start-ups and market leaders, to engine their new products 2 times faster than an in-house development team."

REMEMBER: THE KEY IS TO CONNECT, ENGAGE AND STIMULATE INTEREST. DO THAT BY BEING CLEAR, SIMPLE AND COMPELLING BECAUSE IT'S ABOUT THEM, NOT YOU.

COACHING EXERCISE 14: Craft Your "Elevated" Ingredients

Write your Elevated Ingredients. You've created all of the ingredients already in many of the Coaching Exercises you've already completed. You'll bring them together here.

1. For (Your Ideal Customer)

_____

_____

_____

_____

2. Who Is: (State the Problem They Want to Solve)

_____

_____

_____

3. I Am: (Your Field and Super Power)

_____

_____

_____

4. That: (Key Problem-solving Ability)

_____

_____

_____

5. Delivering: (Their Aspirations)

_____

_____

_____

Next write a few paragraphs using the other three Super Powers you've identified. Those three also make you different. Even though they're not as strong as the one you choose for your Hook sentence, they'll help you weave a really strong story. They become your key messages built on the things that make you different. Now you have your "About Us" copy for your website and brochure.

Here's what our Dr. K wrote with her other ideas:

- "For women who want a primary physician with a natural approach to menopause and women's health concerns, Dr. K is "The Listening Doctor" who gets to the root cause of your problems."

- A medically trained, licensed naturopathic physician, Dr. K seeks natural solutions to tackle the cause of health imbalances and to avoid dangerous side effects, using prescription medications only as the situation warrants.

- Whether you're dealing with raging hormones, fatigue, excess weight, or visible signs of aging, it's time to work with someone who really listens to you and spends time with you. Working with Dr. K, you'll naturally return to the "me" you used to be.

Once you've chosen just the right words to convey your unique message, then practice, practice, practice saying it until it feels like an integral part of you. Test it out on strangers, people who know you, as well as your customers and see what sort of response you get. Do they look fascinated, intrigued, curious? If so, you're on the right track. Do they look baffled, confused, or dazed? If so, ask for some feedback, re-work your message and try again.

Do not show people your Elevated Ingredients or drafted Hook and ask, "I'm working on the Hook for my business—what do you think of this?" It's much better to try your message out on them and see what happens rather than to talk "about" it. They want to help. They just don't know how because they haven't been through these steps with you.

TO TAGLINE OR NOT TO TAGLINE

By the end of building your Hook, you'll be feeling confident and clear about the language you'll use to communicate what you do (your Super Power) that's excessively important to your Ideal Customer. This is the time when a tagline might pop its head out, some clever or catchy way to capture your unique Hook.

We've noticed business owners tend to obsess and worry about having the "perfect" tagline; they lose sleep and sometimes feel they can't move forward until they find the "Just Do It," "It's The Real Thing" or the "When it absolutely, positively has to be there overnight" phrase to capture the essence of their business message. We're here to alleviate your concerns.

We think of taglines as "a spice in the soup" or the "cherry on the top" of your Hook: nice but not critical. If you stumble on a good tagline, fab. Often taglines emerge over time. If you don't have one, no worries. You don't have to have one. Plenty of highly successful businesses operate without one. You can too. Trust one will arrive when it's ready to show its face. In the meantime, keep moving forward with your Hook.

HOOK INSECURITY

Thinking, mulling, pondering, writing, scratching out, redoing and finally settling on your Super Power and Hook, frankly, will try your soul. Martha likens it to a surgeon performing an operation on himself...and without anesthesia. It's challenging to be so immersed in your business and also step outside and examine it objectively.

● ● ● ● ● ● ● ● ● ● ● ● ● ● ● ● **SALES SIDEBAR**

Did your brain just explode from working to see yourself as others see you? To figure out your Super Power, Hook and then Elevated Ingredients? Yeah, it's hard. We fully admit it. An objective, freshly, trained eye from an outsider might be just the ticket. We frequently create Elevated Ingredients and Hook statements for our customers. We interview you, sometimes a few of your customers, take an objective look at your business, uncover the places where you're being too humble and craft the entire Super Power-Hook-Elevated Ingredients-About Us-copy for you. If you'd like us to help, give us a call. There we go... selling again. Why? Because you don't have to be in this alone. It's our responsibility to tell you. And it's your responsibility to tell your customers, too.

WHY PEOPLE CHOOSE ONE BRAND VERSUS ANOTHER

Martha loves to ask this question when she's speaking at events or doing webinars:

"What type of car do you drive?"

The answer isn't important, really. It doesn't matter if you say Ford or Ferrari. The real reason she asks the question is the learning the question (and, yes, there is an answer...just not that one above) embeds: **no one is ever driving the least expensive car (or truck) on the market.**

Her next question:

"Why don't you drive the least expensive car on the market?"

The answer is always the same…"because the car I choose offered the value I was looking for."

The Ford owners felt Ford offered the most value. The Ferrari owners (don't think there have been any of those) believe Ferrari offers the most value. The Toyota owners feel Toyota is the best way for them to go and so on.

How did all these people figure out what product delivered the value they wanted? And they were so convinced the value was so pluperfect for them, they went out and bought a car/truck that wasn't the cheapest on the market.

VALUE TRUMPS PRICE.

The methodology they used should create a startling realization for you:

Value trumps price.

Value trumps price, my friends. The perception of value is the reason people do not buy the cheapest item on the market. If you're struggling with putting a legitimate price on your services or hear "you're too expensive," we're about to show you how to put that struggle to an end.

What is value and how do you convey it?

VALUE: IT'S ALL IN THE MIND OF YOUR BEHOLDER

A bit ago, Martha was on the phone working with a client. The client was working on why her initial offer wasn't attracting the number of customers she anticipated.

"Tell me the value of working with you," Martha said. "What is the outcome of working with you?"

"Well, my product is the best on the market," she said.

"That's nice, but it doesn't tell me anything. Not only does everybody say that, nobody cares about your product, at least not now. Your customer doesn't care about your product, or that it's the best on the market," Martha replied. "What happens when someone works with you? What is their outcome? How do they transform?"

Crickets.

The client was speechless. She had no idea what her value was to her customer except in the context of the product she offered.

She's not alone. Way too many businesses work really hard at getting their customers to understand *them.* That's the problem.

We should be working really hard to *understand our customer.*

WORK HARD TO UNDERSTAND YOUR CUSTOMER, NOT TO HAVE YOUR CUSTOMER UNDERSTAND YOU.

Your **#1 job** as the marketer/seller in your business is to **understand what your customer is thinking, have insights into their mind**. Right? We've already talk at length about this. Well, it applies to the value you bring, also.

And how your Ideal Customer perceives value centers on them, too. Not you.

Your Ideal Customer perceives value by considering how to make their life better, solve a problem or meet a desire. You take away a headache or make something good great. Remember: your Ideal Customer isn't thinking about you. They are thinking about what you can do for them, how you change them, how you eliminate their headache or make their life better.

That's your value.

It's like a before-and-after photo. The value in working with you is how they transform from the person in the "photo" on the left to the person in the "photo" on the right.

Your job requires you to clearly spell out what value looks like in your hands. *If you don't tell your prospect, they'll decide for themselves.* Truth be told your Ideal Prospect is highly likely to be wrong about the value of working with you.

CLARITY ALWAYS TRUMPS PERSUASION.

The job rests with you to create the perceived value of working with you. Share your value. Be crystal clear about your value. Don't leave your customer to figure it out or decode it. They won't. Clarity always trumps persuasion. Always.

Thankfully, the way to express your value can be identified by meeting four criteria. Here's what your value statement must do to get a "yes" from your prospect:

• Your prospect must say "I want it." Think Attraction.

- Your prospect must say "I really can't get this anywhere else." Think Uniqueness.

- Your prospect must say "I understand your offer/you." Think Clarity.

- Your prospect must say "I believe your offer/you." Think Credibility.

Ready for some pondering to find your answers? Frankly, if you've tackled the *Coaching Exercises* to this point in the book, you have most of the answers. We're suggesting you do them again here (or refine what you wrote originally because you're much more in the swing of it now) to align them to your value statements. This is your guideline for readiness to share your value.

Are you in the right-headed space to give someone an accurate and compelling stroll through your value?

COACHING EXERCISE 15: *Express Your Value*

If you don't tell your Ideal Customers the value of working with you, who will? They will make up your value, and odds are they won't be accurate. This exercise will enable you to determine your value so you can share it for the benefit of your Ideal Customer (they'll know) and you (it will be correct).

1. Your Ideal Customer must want it. Think Attraction. How do you attract customers (remember what you created in the **Think Like Your Customer** *Coaching Exercises*)?

_____

_____

_____

_____

_____

_____

2. Your Ideal Customer must believe they cannot get it elsewhere. Think uniqueness. What about you is unique in a way your Ideal Customer covets (This is your Super Power. Look at the *Coaching Exercise* you did above)?

_____

_____

_____

_____

_____

3. Your Ideal Customer must understand your offer/you. Think Clarity. Write down your offer, without using professional language (and remember your offer is you solve their problem).

_____

_____

_____

_____

4. Your Ideal Customer must believe your offer/you. Think credibility. Write down your offer without using hype or tried-and-true-heard-it-all-before language.

_____

_____

_____

_____

_____

Now put it into action. Say it when you meet people or when you speak from the stage. Put it on your website and marketing brochures. Train your contractors and employees about your value so they can share it with your customers and prospects, too.

Never assume your customers will understand your value. Tell them clearly. That how Ford sells Fords and Ferrari sells Ferraris.

YOU SELL. YOUR CUSTOMERS BUY.

When you stop to think about it, buying and selling aren't the same thing at all, are they? Whether you use a formal, informal or totally random process for selling, your Ideal Customer doesn't follow your process at all as they go about the act of buying.

Let me give you an example. A few years ago Martha decided it was time to upgrade to a road bike. She wanted a new bike because she was starting to do some fun bike races and her heavier hybrid bike made it more difficult to motor up the hills (plus, she didn't think it was as cool looking as a road bike, the favored bike of "serious" bikers; can you say her ego got a little involved?). That's how Martha was defining her problem: ride more easily and quickly in fun races, quit laboring at the back of the pack and look cooler than she believed she currently was looking.

Next, Martha went on-line to look at a few bikes. She already had a favorite brand, the brand of her hybrid. She investigated many road bikes by that manufacturer, checked out a couple of other brands "just in case" they were better than she thought, read the reviews and made sure the road bike prices fit her budget. She educated herself, discovered what she wanted.

She packed up her info and walked into the local bike store. She showed the sales guy who approached her the bike information she had accumulated. He pulled both bikes and rattled off the features of each. He made it his business to educate her about each bike.

Then he began to validate her choice of bikes. He told her why each was a wise purchase. They had great reviews and low maintenance requirements. He shared how each had the features in a road bike she wanted, and each would last her for years. He justified the bikes prices by sharing their bike servicing policy and how it would keep Martha and the bike on the road without needing to upgrade.

Finally, he validated that one of the bikes was the best choice and fit her budget.

His selling process was:

- Educate

- Validate

- Justify

Yet, Martha didn't buy. The whole transaction seemed focused on the bike features, and it felt like what he wanted was to make a sale. He wasn't pushy. He wasn't obnoxious. He just didn't seem to be very engaged with Martha. She moved on.

Then she headed into her favorite bike shop to check out the two bikes that passed her investigation. When she got to the store, she made a bee line to the first bike and hovered, checking out the bike overall (and the color...color was important). One of the sales guys came over and after a bit of discussion he asked her what was encouraging her to get a road bike when she had just bought a hybrid so recently. She shared her problem. He pulled out the first bike on here list and offered her to give it a test ride. With helmet on and a fast sizing so the pedals were in the right place, she headed out for a short spin. Meh. Not so exciting as it felt too much like her hybrid, not the upgrade she was hoping for.

Back to the store she pedaled. The sales guy pulled out the second bike her research indicated would fit the bill. Again, she headed out for a test ride, and again, she was unimpressed. Just another bike too similar to the one she already had.

The sales guy did something special. He asked Martha why she wanted to upgrade from a hybrid to a road bike. She shared her desire to ride faster, not pedal at the back of the pack during fun rides and enjoy the feel of a lighter, more "seriously professional" bike.

He nodded and pulled out a bike she hadn't researched. "Take this for a ride," he said. "I think it will deliver what you're looking for."

Out Martha went on a ride. And...OMG...what a bike. It was smooth. It was fast. It fit her like a glove. She was kind of liking this bike. More than liking it. Loving it. She wanted to own it, which was frankly her next step in her buying process...owning it, as in "I have to have it."

But wait a minute! This wonderful, comfortable, swift, beautiful (it was purple and white) bike was TWICE THE PRICE of the two bikes she came in to investigate and buy. Twice!!

Rationalization kicked in. "It's everything I want in a bike. It's fast. It's light weight. It will enable me to tackle my problem of being at the back of the pack in fun races. It's comfortable, easy to handle and it's a very cool color." Martha was busy doing what so many of us do when we want something that solves our problem. She was busy rationalizing.

Of course, you know the end of this story. The bike went home with Martha, and they've been living happily ever after.

Here was Martha's buying process:

- First, she recognized her problem. She wanted a faster, more comfortable bike and it had to be a road bike because she was tired of biking with the slow pokes at the back of the pack, not looking "cool" enough, in her opinion

- Next, she went on line and educated herself about road bikes

- Then she rode a few and found one she was kind of loving (because the bike sales guy gave her an assignment...would you be willing to try this bike?). She began to "own" it.

- Last, despite the higher price...much higher price...yeah, it was a lot higher priced...she rationalized owning it. "I have to have it because..."

- It took away her pain

That was Martha's buying process, and it's a pretty good representation of how all of us buy: define our problem, educate ourselves, find something we like and begin to "own" it and then rationalize the purchase. So now you also know why you often buy things more expensive than you intended. The purchase "suited" you.

If that's how we buy, let's examine that process versus how we sell.

Let's go back to the sales approach of the first bike store sales guy.

- Educate

- Validate

- Justify

Now compare that to the sales process with the second bike store sales guy.

He began his conversation by educating Martha about the bikes. All the features, yes, but more importantly how each bike solved her problem. He began his sales approach with education. The education was about seeking out the problem she wanted to solve. The bike that solved Martha's problem the best was the last bike she rode, the one he pulled out to fit her problem-solving criteria rather than either of the two bikes she came in to ride and buy.

Next, he validated the choice of the more expensive bike. Yes, it was sleek. Yes, it was a comfortable ride. And most importantly, yes, it was faster, lighter and easier to move you to the middle of the fun ride bike pack rather than hanging out at the rear end.

Finally, he justified the purchase. It's super cool. You look great on it, and it solves your problem.

His selling process matched Martha's buying process:

- Discover and educate

- Own it (even gave her an assignment...ride them)

- Rationalize it

- Decide

HOW CAN YOU ADJUST YOUR SELLING PROCESS TO MATCH YOUR IDEAL CUSTOMER'S BUYING PROCESS?

His selling process and Martha's buying process were a perfect match. In the first store, no purchase occurred. The sales guy was feature-oriented rather than problem-solving oriented. Plus, he never pulled out a bike for her to ride. In the second store, the sales guy aligned his selling process to better match Martha's unconscious buying process.

By the way, there was nothing unusual about Martha's buying process. It's the way most of us buy, even if we're unaware we even have a process.

The question to you is this...how can you adjust how you sell to better match how your Ideal Customer buys?

Your Ideal Customer isn't going to line up with your sales approach. They have their own way of getting to a buying decision. You get to choose. Either go your own way and make the sale...or not; or recognize your selling process could use a little adjustment to better align with how your Ideal Customer makes buying decisions.

Not a tough choice if you think about it.

As you begin your conversation with an Ideal Prospect, you're very first requirement discovers the problem they believe they have...not the problem you know they have. What they want, rather than what you...as the professional...know they need.

If your questioning cannot find the problem they are committed to solving...because there are problems you might uncover they are happy to live with...take the questions a different direction. When you have identified their driving problem, you can then focus on aligning to how they decide. They will want you to educate them about their problem and how you can make it go away...the outcome of working with you rather than the solution you offer. When you are offering them something so good they cannot resist, you'll watch them begin to own the solution. They have to have it. Cannot let it go. They will begin to rationalize working with you, taking you up on your offer. And the next thing you know, you'll have a credit card in your hand.

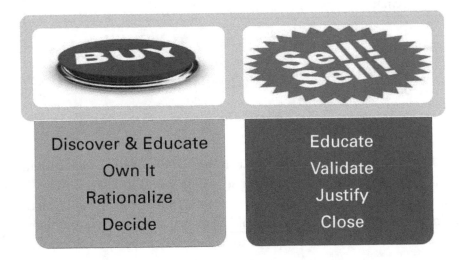

Yes, it might not be that swift or straight-forward. However, recognizing the buying and selling are two different paths will only serve you and your Ideal Customer to come together.

You see the issue? You're approaching your Ideal Customer with a process that doesn't match their defacto process? You're pulling right; they're moving left.

What would happen to you if you adopted a Buying Process rather than a Selling Process?

ADOPTING A BUYING PROCESS

What would it look like...in the real world...to transform from a selling process to a buying process? We've already worked through several adjustments in earlier Sections. This is just one more example of acting like your customer.

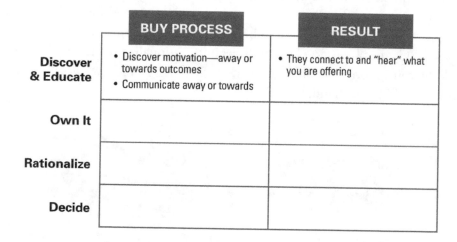

	BUY PROCESS	RESULT
Discover & Educate	• Discover motivation—away or towards outcomes • Communicate away or towards	• They connect to and "hear" what you are offering
Own It		
Rationalize		
Decide		

The first step aids your Ideal Customer in discovering your eliminate their pain. Educate them that you see their world as they see it. When you communicate from their Buying Motivation perspective—away from pain or towards pleasure—your Ideal Customer can "hear" you through the noise of the market. Your Step 1 is to deliver **Discover and Educate**.

	BUY PROCESS	RESULT
Discover & Educate	• Discover motivation—away or towards outcomes • Communicate away or towards	• They connect to and "hear" what you are offering
Own It	• Give them an assignment • Ask cause/effect questions	• Begin transfer of ownership to them from you • 2 buyers, different motivators
Rationalize		
Decide		

The next step in your Ideal Customer's Buying Process steps them into the **Own It** stage. You want to turn over the ownership of the relief from pain from you to your Ideal Customer. Think of it this way. You are far more likely driven to make a sale than your Ideal Customer is to buy. You are fully owning the outcome because you know...it your heart and soul... you really, really, really can make their life better. You're all in. Your Ideal Prospect might not even have a toe in. When your Ideal Prospect gets so excited about getting out of their situation, they begin to see themselves without their pain. They start to feel a sense of "ownership" in what you're offering them. Think of Martha and her road bike. She came into the store to buy one of two bikes she had researched. But then she got on a third bike...one she decided solved her problem...and she fell in love with Bike #3. She began to "own" that bike while she was still out on a test ride.

Can you see the subtle, yet effective way ownership began to shift from the bike sales guy to Martha? He gave her an assignment, a small one. Ride this bike. Executing the assignment dropped Martha squarely into feeling what it would be like to ride faster, to not spend her time at the back of the fun ride pack. She loved that feeling and didn't want to let it go. That meant holding tightly to the bike!

A small assignment, something your Ideal Prospect is willing to do, begins to show them what it feels like to be rid of the problem or reinforces the pain they are experiencing. And they won't want to let that feeling go either, or they'll have more urgency in ridding themselves of their problem.

Ah Ha Moment ⚡: PETRA AND EDWARD

Petra and Edward own a financial business, offering nano-sized loans to small businesses. Working with Martha they created two ways to move ownership from them to their Ideal Customer. They created two different types of small assignments. As they asked questions and began to understand the Ideal Prospect in front of them, Petra and Edward would ask the Ideal Prospect if they would be willing to do a very small assignment.

The first assignment they offered was: would you be willing to write down all the things in your business you could now buy because you have nano-loan money? The Ideal Prospect almost always said "yes." Then Petra and Edward would ask: would you then be willing to send us your list? Again, the Ideal Prospect almost always agreed. Finally, Petra and Edward would ask: can we schedule our next call to discuss what's on your list? And, again, the Prospect almost always said "yes" to the next appointment.

Look what just happened here. I hope it blew your mind.

The assignment puts the Ideal Prospect in the mindset of "these things are possible where they haven't been possible in the past!" Do you believe the Prospect will want to emotionally surrender those purchases which will improve their business? They just experienced the feeling of relief from their money concerns. They had a few minutes to sit in a very exciting place, the place where their problem goes away, and they attain what they've wanted. Surrender those feelings? Probably not. They want them and don't really want to hand them back. They experienced what the relief from pain would actually feel like.

Second, Petra and Edward secured the next appointment without feeling like they were pushy. The next appointment became easy to set.

This is the first of the two different approaches to offering an Assignment Martha, Petra and Edward devised. Here's the second.

With some clients Petra and Edward would take a different approach. Instead of asking if they would be willing to do an Assignment that enabled the Ideal Prospect to experience relief from their pain, they would offer a small Assignment that accentuated the pain.

This assignment looked like this: would you be willing to write down all the things in your business you've postponed buying and the team you've been unable to bring in because you haven't had sufficient funds?

While the Assignment request was different, the rest of the conversation proceeded as above. They asked if the Ideal Prospect would send them the list, and then requested the next appointment to discuss what was on the list.

This second type of Assignment plopped the Prospect squarely into the depths of their problem. The Assignment drew the pain forward and made the Prospect acutely aware. Now the Prospect was eager to own the path out of their situation.

Petra and Edward used two different Assignment approaches simply to see which one created the best sense of ownership. Two years later, we can share there is no "best" approach as both have been producing wonderful results for Petra, Edward and their Ideal Customers. Petra and Edward must decide as they talk to their Prospect which Assignment to offer, which one they believe is more in alignment with their Ideal Prospect.

You don't have to create two Assignments. Simply start with one either focusing on the relief from pain your Ideal Prospect will experience when they work with you or the accentuation of pain they'll experience if they remain in their current situation.

To support your growing ability to turn ownership over to your Ideal Prospect ask great cause-and-effect questions. The answers to cause-and-effect questions squeezes out what's driving your Ideal Prospect. Their responses to these questions will show you the problem they want to solve, giving you the insight to turn your conversation towards their problem as they see it.

Cause-and-effect questions can look like this:

- What's causing you to look for xxx?

- What is your sense of urgency to get new results?

- What is the impact/payback that you expect when you solve your problem?

- What are the consequences of staying in your current state?

The cause part of these questions enables you to see their motivators to do something. The effect element fleshes out the fall-out those drivers generate. Cause-and-effect questions help you identify and organize what's rolling through the head of your Ideal Prospect. You have information to talk to your Ideal Prospect in a systematic and logical...and emotional way...about their issue. The questions permit your Ideal Prospect to hear the issues when they say them out loud which usually accentuates their recognition of their unacceptable situation.

You and your Ideal Prospect will see the root causes of their problem. Their answers to the questions encourage discussion and offer you an opportunity to show off your wisdom about the problem. If the cause-and-effect questions haven't resulted in a fleshing out of the problem, adjust your questions. Your Ideal Prospect will not be in action to relieve their issue until you've uncovered the exact nature of the problem they no longer want to live with.

These offer only a few examples of the types of cause-and-effect questions you can ask your Ideal Prospect.

	BUY PROCESS	RESULT
Discover & Educate	• Discover motivation—away or towards outcomes • Communicate away or towards	• They connect to and "hear" what you are offering
Own It	• Give them an assignment • Ask cause/effect questions	• Begin transfer of ownership to them from you • 2 buyers, different motivators
Rationalize	• Show how you take away pain or move towards pleasure	• Create value from their perspective
Decide		

Your Ideal Prospect's next step in their unconscious Buying Process means they begin to **Rationalize** the purchase. You're now creating value from your Ideal Prospect's perspective. What does value look like for them? Your service features offer no value. At least not yet. Value equals how their life changes when they work with you. Remember how you build perceived value:

- Your prospect must say "I want it." Think Attraction.

- Your prospect must say "I really can't get this anywhere else." Think Uniqueness.

- Your prospect must say "I understand your offer/you." Think Clarity.

- Your prospect must say "I believe your offer/you." Think Credibility.

Value signifies you're the finest source for removing their pain. When you focus on building value from your Ideal Customer's perspective, you'll see the world through their eyes, and they'll see the path through your expert direction.

	BUY PROCESS	RESULT
Discover & Educate	• Discover motivation—away or towards outcomes • Communicate away or towards	• They connect to and "hear" what you are offering
Own It	• Give them an assignment • Ask cause/effect questions	• Begin transfer of ownership to them from you • 2 buyers, different motivators
Rationalize	• Show how you take away pain or move towards pleasure	• Create value from their perspective
Decide	• Reinforce solution removes pain or delivers pleasure	• You stayed in control • They buy more

The last step in your journey of moving to a Buying Process, your Ideal Prospect's last step, is the **Decide** step. What does it take for them to decide on you? It takes your reinforcement that you remove their pain they want to go away or move them towards the pleasure they seek.

Moving through the Buying Process steps to the "here's my credit card" step will likely take a number of engagements, either through email, phone conversations or in-persona meetings. You might experience a shorten time to sale. Or it takes just as long. You might experience more sales. In the end whether it takes a minute or hundreds of minutes, you'll make more sales recognizing and using your Ideal Prospect's Buying Process (even though they have no idea they have and use such a process).

Will every Prospect buy from you when you move to a Buying Process? Of course, not. Will more people buy? Of course, they will because you've gotten out of your mind and into the minds of your Ideal Customer. You're acting like they act, thinking like they think. You're entering Customertopia.

....
COACHING EXERCISE 16: *Build Your Buying Process*

1. What's the pain your Ideal Customer wants to move away from or the pleasure they want to move towards?

_____

_____

_____

_____

2. Design an Assignment you can offer your Ideal Prospect to enable ownership of the decision to move from you to them?

_____

_____

_____

_____

3. Return to your *Coaching Exercise on Value.* How did you state your Value, so it aligns with what your Ideal Customer values?

_____

_____

_____

_____

4. List five cause-and-effect questions you can ask your Ideal Prospects to help you and them unearth their problem.

1. _____

2. _____

3. _____

4. _____

5. _____

It's your turn. Give it a try. Identify a few Ideal Prospects who have yet to say "yes" to you. Reopen a conversation with them. Ask them if they would be willing to do a small Assignment. And send it to you by an agreed date. Set up a follow-up appointment to discuss what they created in the Assignment.

Record your results. How many did the Assignment? Did the Assignment shift ownership to your Ideal Prospect? And if so, how many people sent you their Assignment as agreed and kept the next appointment with you?

THE LAST GOTCHA

As you begin to think and act like your Ideal Customer, there's one last area for examination and discussion, one final spot where you can accidently fall out of alignment with your Ideal Customer.

In the Discovery and Education process, your Ideal Customers begin to develop an opinion of what they *want* to solve their pain issue. They begin to form an idea of what they want. They become alert to ads, Facebook posts, conversations and other forms of marketing that talk about delivering what they want. But they are not experts in the removal of their pain (if they were experts, they would have removed the pain and moved on to something else). So many times, what they want really won't solve

THEY *WANT* SOMETHING. YOU KNOW THEY *NEED* SOMETHING ELSE.

their pain. Yet, it's what their ears can hear, and their eyes can see. It's all they know.

You, on the other hand, are the expert. You fully grasp what they *need* to eliminate their pain. Most times what they want and what you know they need are completely different things.

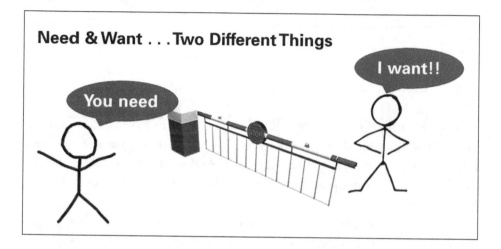

The danger in this difference shows up when you begin to market and sell. You've accidently created friction in your marketing and sales system. Friction anywhere in your marketing and sales approach injects resistance. Friction creates conflict, a clash of wills...yours versus your Ideal Customer. You didn't intend to create friction but need versus want does just that.

If you're talking about what people need and it doesn't match what they want, your Ideal Customer cannot hear you or see you. Your message falls flat or worse, doesn't even make a sound. The sound of one hand clapping. Not good.

On the other hand, you have integrity and never want to sell something to someone not in their best interests.

How can you navigate this conflict?

Attract them to you with what they *want,* and as you begin conversations, show them what they *need* and why.

At Wide Awake Business, we often have people call us to discuss building a website for them. They want a website because they know their business must have one to be considered valid and real. We'll ask them questions about their Ideal Customer (you've read this far so you know what the questions look like). We inquire about the problem their Ideal Customer has. We poke around to determine their Super Powers. If the Ideal Customer has none of this in place, we would be out of integrity to sell them a website. The site might be pretty, but the copy written and pictures chosen wouldn't speak to the visitor. That's nothing but a waste of money, and that's not part of our values. We never want to waste a Indian-head nickel of your money.

We'll have a conversation with them about what they need before they spend money on what they want. What they need is for us to first work with them to identify everything we've discussed in the **Part 2: Think Like Your Customer** Section. When we've created those insights about their Ideal Customer, only then can we begin work on the website. If the Ideal Customer is on-board with our expert recommendation, off we go to work together. If they aren't, if they really just want a website, then they aren't our Ideal Customer. Our company values would not permit us to sell something if it's not the right thing to sell.

The difference between want and need trips up many businesses. Just another small adjustment on your part to become customer-centered and enter Customertopia.

COACHING EXERCISE 17: Customer Wants versus Needs

1. What does your Ideal Customer want? What are they looking for?

_____

_____

_____

_____

_____

_____

2. As the expert, what do you know they need?

_____

_____

_____

_____

_____

3. Map out your plan to bridge the scary gap between what they want and what you know they need...so they can hear and see your marketing and respond and you're not talking about needs they don't recognize or value.

_____

_____

_____

_____

4. Review all your marketing materials, your website copy, brochures and anything else you use. What materials require changes to align with what your Ideal Customer wants?

_____

_____

_____

_____

_____

5. What will you say now to align to what they want rather than simply what they need?

_____

_____

_____

_____

_____

_____

Let's be super clear. Want versus need doesn't mean you must stop communicating what your Ideal Customer needs. It does mean you begin to communicate what they want. Otherwise, you'll be as lonely as the Maytag repairman (remember those commercials?).

Remember, all these Coaching Exercises are available to you, along with special offers on our website: wideawakebusiness.com/resources

---

PART FOUR

Build Your Customer Machine

I magine today is Saturday, and you've got a long list of errands to run. The places you must drive to are all over town. You start tackling all your errands, driving from one store to the next. You head to the paint store for a gallon of Quietude to paint the bathroom. Next, you motor over to the other end of town to grab a great deal on socks at Target, and then on to have the car washed which is located very near the paint store. Wait...you were just here. You could have picked up the paint and then the socks and then gone to the car wash. And the grocery store, next on your list, should be last because you're buying ice cream, and it will melt by the time you make your last stop at the gas station which isn't near the grocery store either.

Your Saturday motoring had no plan, no pre-thought-out direction. You got in the car and went and discovered if you had just taken a few minutes to map out your destinations, you could have been more efficient with your time. You were substantially less than machine-like in your execution of your Saturday errands.

Let's turn this example a different direction...towards how you've built your business. You've gone to conferences, hired experts, read books, used your business background (if you have one), all in an effort to make money. Those conferences, experts and books likely told you that to find Ideal Prospects you must be on Facebook, LinkedIn, Twitter, Instagram, maybe

Pinterest, have a website and a landing page or four, write a blog, record a podcast, create a vlog, get out and network, join organizations, write a book, hold a webinar, create affiliations to build your database, do radio interviews, get out and speak at events and call, call, call.

We hear you laughing. But you're laughing because you know that's all true!

You went out and did much or all of it. Yet, your business did not improve, or at least not as much as you predicted or hoped.

The reason your business didn't explode with new Ideal Customers centers around a simple reality...all of that was just a random list of "stuff." All action with few results. All the stuff made you busy. It didn't make you successful.

Fundamentally, your business was randomly "driving around town," running errands without a thought-out plan. Your attempts to attract more Ideal Customers ran into the buzz saw of three problems.

RANDOM BAD. MACHINE GOOD.

Problem #1 in your approach to building and growing your business stems from the unpredictability of how your business is structured. The strategies, approaches and actions you've chosen might be in place because they suit you. They might be in place just because it was the next idea to come down the pike. They might be in place because someone told you these actions are sure to work for you, yet they didn't know much about your business. Likely nothing really links together, like driving all over town to complete your errands.

MACHINES CREATE PROCESS OUT OF RANDOM ACTIONS.

In other words, every day is a new day unlike the day before.

Machines, on the other hand, create process out of random actions. Machines reduce the burden of what comes next, taking some of the thinking out of actions. Machines, within our business, create a more mature company. Machines take work off your plate and put time back in your day.

Then **Problem #2** pops up. All machines do not deliver equally. Some create the desired results, more customers and more business. Some just rearrange the deck chairs on the Titanic, as they say.

Most business owners with a machine-like business built it based on what works for them. You look at the toil on your plate and determine the best way to get it off your plate. You follow the lead of alleged "experts" who tell you what you should be doing to get more customers, make more money and have more time for yourself. You organize for you.

Here comes **Problem #3**. The way you've organized your business doesn't match how your Ideal Customer operates. At best, you have some willing Ideal Prospects prepared to work with your "machine" because you're delivering something they want dearly, they are your sister's husband's brother-in-law. At the most awful, you've accidently created friction, and they cannot engage.

Accidental friction occurs because you've set up your business strategies, structure, processes and actions to work for *you*. While we absolutely want your machine to work for you, a machine built for your Ideal Customer is just as important. Building the structure of your business in a way that suites your Ideal Customer enables them to engage with you the way *they* prefer, where they prefer and how they prefer. These might not be conscious preferences on the part of your Ideal Customer. But preferences they are.

MACHINES BUILT FOR CUSTOMERS DELIVER SUPERIOR RESULTS TO MACHINES BUILT FOR YOU.

Building or for many adjusting for your Ideal Customer activates your business. You're ready for new leads who become Ideal Prospects...who transform into new Ideal Customers...and more revenue. In **Part Four: Build For Your Customer**, we'll figure out your best way to build or adjust your business machine to turn it into a Customer Machine, what strategies, techniques and actions you keep, which you toss aside and what new ones you will create. Strategies and actions that started your business may need to be replaced with those better suited to how your Ideal Customer works and plays.

YOUR PROGRESS SO FAR

If you're feeling just a little overwhelmed by the idea of adjusting your business machine, perhaps the moment is right to recap how much you've uncovered about your Ideal Customer, which, when you implement what you already know, will blow up any customer attraction logjams you might be experiencing.

You've got the foundational requirements of your business firmly in place. You've learned to think like your Ideal Customer and act like your Ideal Customer. Now, start to put these changes in place, these first steps of *Customertopia*. You don't have to wait until you've read and absorbed everything in this book to be in action. Action can happen with every page you read. Because guess what would be happening for you right now if you did? Customers would be paying more attention to you with some saying "yes" faster than you've experienced in the past. That would feel as good as a vacation to the warm, sunny, relaxing Hawaiian Islands. Maybe it would pay for the Hawaiian Islands trip.

Success tastes succulent, luscious and delicious. Your first yummy thrill encourages the next wallet-plumping nibble, and the next and the next.

Okay, breath taken. You truly are ready for your next step on the road to your *Customertopia*.

Your next success morsel comes by *building a business machine to fit your customer,* a Customer Machine. Your own Customer Machine does require a bit of housekeeping because you'll be reconstructing your business to take out the friction you likely have in engaging with customers. Accidental friction. But friction, nonetheless.

What do we mean by a Machine?

A machine has several parts, each with a definite function, working together to perform a specific task. Machines enable a business to achieve high volume, detailed organization of material flow, careful control of quality standards, efficient division of labor and the repeated delivery of consistent, repeatable results.

The machine you'll build for your business manifests as a Customer-focused Machine generating improved results...a continuous, predictable flow of customers and revenue to your business and your wallet. We talk about building the machine for your customer because customers fuel your success, power essential to keep your business running and growing. Without customers, your business grinds to a standstill.

Want to see a little "customer machine" in action? Here's a small glimpse into Chris' family Machine.

AH HA MOMENT ⚡: CHRIS

Winter was coming. It does, every year. Chris and her family know that, yet somehow it sneaks up on them all the same. Time to chop and stack wood to keep them toasty warm through the winter. Yes, they have a furnace, but the warmth from a wood stove feels so wonderful. When it's time to build the wood pile, it's all hands on-deck. Family Chris has a plan. They have a system...a firewood generating machine.

From the youngest to the oldest, everybody has a job. Grandpa finds the fallen trees and clears the path. Maybe he cuts down a dead tree that hasn't fallen yet. Mom uses the chain saw to cut the tree into manageable chunks. Not too big, not too small. The right size for the chopping block.

Oldest child has splitting duty. She puts her whole body into the swing and gets frustrated if the log doesn't split all the way on the first pass. Two middle children load the wheelbarrow, aiming for a perfect load...enough to make the trip worth it, but not so much the barrow becomes impossible to push. When the wheelbarrow is full, they take turns rolling to the patio where the wood pile stands. Sometimes it takes them both, an exercise in cooperation.

At the patio, the youngest has unloading duty, taking the logs one at a time and carefully building the stack. When she gets impatient, the middle two unload and then return to build the next load.

A perfect machine. Everybody has a job suited to their ability, and one job can't start until the one before it is completed. To be efficient, jobs must be synchronized, or somebody stands idle for too long while someone else feels overloaded. Family Chris has a pretty good estimate of how much wood they'll need (with a little help from *Farmer's Almanac* predicting how cold the winter will be). When they reach their targeted amount, they do an extra load or two, just for good measure.

When the task is finished, their little machine has done its job. They've worked together and have what they need to be warm all winter. A Family Machine built to keep them cozy.

Now imagine your business running like a Machine. Everyone has a responsibility suited to their ability and the needs of your Ideal Customer. You know the order in which each task must be completed to keep the Machine in motion, best attract and engage Ideal Prospects, never suffer an idle person and nary someone overloaded (especially you). When you begin to build your business like a Machine...a Machine aligned with how your Ideal Customer operates...you have a Customer-making Machine on your hands!

TURN ON YOUR CUSTOMER MACHINE

Customers provide the foundation of your business success. Of course. Without them, you simply don't have a business. You have a hobby. And you want more than a hobby. You're already dedicated to your business and its success. So...unless you plan to work 24 hours a day, 7 days a week, you must have a system...a Customer Machine... to attract Ideal Prospects and turn them into Ideal Customers.

UNTIL YOUR CUSTOMER-ATTRACTING PROCESS BECOMES SYSTEMATIZED, THE ENTIRE BUSINESS PRESSES HEAVILY ON YOUR SHOULDERS ALONE.

Until your customer-attracting process becomes systematized, until you can communicate what must happen regularly when, where and why, the entire business presses heavily on your shoulders alone. No one else can relieve your burden, because they don't know what they should be doing and when. You hold the entire responsibility of putting and keeping the wheels of your business in motion.

You make it happen or it doesn't happen. You. By yourself. All alone. You're the only person who can do it.

Your potential for income, impact and independence expands only as far as what you can do alone. Yet, your potential doubles, triples or quadruples when others put their shoulders into your business... and that demands systems. Business expert Brian Tracy puts it this way, "Your business will be successful, generating steady, predictable sales and cash flow to *the exact degree* to which you develop systems that put as much of your business on autopilot as possible."

Your Customer Machine means your business has a system, a step-by-step process, from beginning to end. A machine that works for you and for your Ideal Customer. You build the system, your machine, to engage as your Ideal Customer requires (more on that shortly). You use the systematized machine to ensure consistent and reliable performance because it works for you *and* for your Ideal Customer.

Your Customer Machine system enables everyone on your Team *and* your Ideal Customer...even if that's just you for the moment...to know what comes next, what happens after that and then the next step to follow that one. When you do the same thing over and over and get the same result, you can train someone else to do the work. When you do the same thing over and over and they are the right things for your Ideal Customer, you will be able to attract and engage with more Ideal Customers. You have created a frictionless system...a Customer Machine. Work becomes easier, simpler and more profitable for you and all the people in your business. Being able to find and engage with you becomes easier, simpler and a happier process for your Ideal Customer.

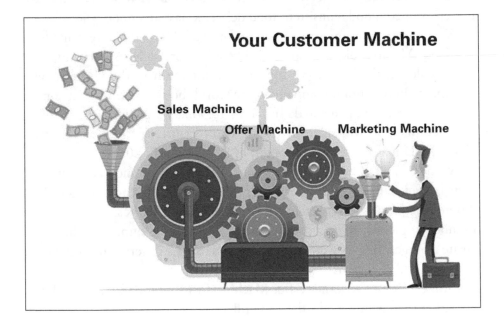

Your Customer Machine can be assembled using from one to three individual machines to create the ultimate in Build for Your Customer Machines:

- Your Customer Marketing Machine: how you attract your Ideal Customer

- Your Customer Offer Machine: what your offer is to your Ideal Customer, and the sequence in which you offer your services

- Your Customer Sales Machine: how you engage with your Ideal Prospect to create and Ideal (paying) Customer

Together, or individually, your ultimate Customer Machines awaits.

MCDONALD'S HAS A LESSON FOR YOU

Ray Kroc, the father of McDonald's as we know it, strongly advocated adherence to the system approach. By focusing on systems first and foremost, McDonald's became an industry leader in franchising their business model. He created the McDonald's system based on what he knew his customers wanted: good, consistent food delivered fast at a good price.

Kroc's system means you can count on a McDonald's burger made in Portland, ME to look, taste and feel like a burger made in Portland, OR. McDonald's is the largest fast-food restaurant chain in the United States and the main restaurant company in the world, both in terms of customers served and revenue generated. In fact, McDonald's could lose half of its sales revenue and still sit in first place comfortably. In the United States alone, McDonald's locations brought in $21 billion in 2018.

Wendy's and Burger King also make hamburgers, and each has their own burger-making Customer Offer Machine. Each cook burgers in a different fashion, squirts ketchup in different amounts, tosses on a diverse number of pickles and finishes it up on a distinctive bun. Yes, they each create a burger. But they create their burgers using a different machine built to attract and engage with their Ideal Customer.

Burger King's Customer Offer Machine focuses on flame-roasted burgers rather than McDonald's flat-top grilled burgers, and they were the first to introduce the concept of "having it your way," leaving off or adding on more of each condiment based on their customer's preferences. Burger King's Customer Offer Machine was designed to attract and engage as their Ideal Customers prefer.

Wendy's very first Customer Offer Machine happened in 1989 when it was the initial company in the industry to introduce a $ .99 Super Value Menu. You can guess the Customer Machine that created! Now they're at it again with their 4 for $4, four items for four bucks. This was more than just another meal deal. Eight sandwiches from which to choose, nuggets, fries and a drink. And a rap song all its own!

You'll notice the McDonald's and Burger King Customer Offer Machines discussed above focus on the product, burgers. The Wendy's Customer Machine we're showcasing here is built on a pricing and bundling machine, a different part of the offer.

YOUR CUSTOMER MACHINE ALREADY EXISTS

Yet, one element of their machines is the same. All three use the same Customer Marketing Machine to attract and engage with customers. They use TV advertising and social media to attract and engage. Each chose this marketing approach because their Ideal Customers watch TV and interact on social media pages. McDonald's, Burger King and Wendy's have built the same Customer Marketing Machines because these methods are proven to work in their industry.

Your industry has a tested, proven method of attracting and engaging with your Ideal Customer, too. You don't have to sit around scratching your head about how you attract more customers...how to market, the nature and sequence of your offer and your method to sell/engage. It's already been done for you. You have role model companies in your industry who have already figured out the best machine for attract Ideal Prospects and turn them into Ideal Customers.

YOU HAVE ROLE MODEL COMPANIES IN YOUR INDUSTRY WHO HAVE ALREADY MAPPED OUT YOUR CUSTOMER MACHINE.

Keep reading as we're going to show you several Customer Machines we've already worked in. One will surely apply to your business. You can thank us later!

As we write this, Wide Awake Business has worked with 5,324 businesses. Our clients include care managers, coaches, consultants, spiritual healers, home remodeling companies, weight-loss specialists, property managers, software developers, residential realtors, court reporters and professional practices such as CPAs, lawyers and veterinarians, to name only a few. Almost all required some type of system for their business, built with their Ideal Customer in the center. Perhaps a system for hiring and training team. Or a system for marketing and selling to their Ideal Customer. Or a system for creating and delivering their programs to their Ideal Customer. Or a system from A to Z.

Each business field comes with its own culture and style, its own way to doing things, its own unique Ideal Customer engagement desires. **How they find, attract and engage with their Ideal Customers represents one of the significant differences**. Therefore, the way each builds their Customer Machines differ.

For example, some businesses such as CPAs and attorneys build their Customer Machine knowing their Ideal Customers prefer to find them by receiving a recommendation from friends and family. These types of businesses acquire most of their business through referrals, and often meeting the provider in person at an event. Product-focused business such as automobile sales or grocers rely on advertising to bring in their Ideal Customers. Shoes, music, clothing and the like is coming to rely on on-line avenues as their Customer Machines. Businesses selling programs, books, webinars, training and such turn to social media advertising and fan pages as their Customer Machine.

YOU DON'T BUILD THE SYSTEM FOR YOUR CONVENIENCE... YOU BUILD IT FOR YOUR CUSTOMER'S EASE.

Some machines often include an offer component. If you've watched a late-night TV commercial for just about anything, their machine relies heavily on their offer. "But, wait! There's more! Get two never-sharpen knives for the same low price. Just pay an additional shipping and handling charge."

Then there are machines constructed wholly or in part with a sales component.

Most Customer Machines are constructed with all three: Customer Marketing Machines, Customer Offer Machines and Customer Sales Machines. Understanding the typical...and yes, successful... path to your Ideal Customer based on what's already working in your industry short-cuts the time required to design your Customer Machine system. A more efficient Customer Machine means you've shortened the time to creating a customer, your Ideal Customer.

AH HA MOMENT ⚡: MARGARET

Margaret owns a coaching practice and created an incredible amount of intellectual property. When we started coaching with her, Margaret barely made $40,000 per year. What's worse, she felt she was under-serving her clients, that she could do so much more for them. Margaret could, indeed, do more for them. To do that, she needed to conquer what was holding her back. Margaret had no system.

Every month, Margaret was basically working hard to create a new "burger." She had no system, and her Ideal Prospects didn't know when she was offering a class, how many classes she was offering in a year or whether they were qualified to take a certain class. She was so inconsistent, it drove her Ideal Prospects crazy, not a great way to endear yourself and create Ideal Customers who want to work with you. We were never surprised to get a call from her saying "Oh my gosh, I have no business this month." She had no system to ensure she would generate revenue on a regular, consistent basis. She hadn't built a Customer Machine that worked for her customer.

Together, we dove in to define a system, a Customer Machine, that worked for Margaret, and more importantly, *worked for her Ideal Prospects.* If Margaret's new Customer Machine only functioned for her…only suited her needs… her Ideal Prospects wouldn't be attracted to the "burger" Margaret put in their hands. They never would become Ideal Customers.

Slowly, Margaret implemented her Customer Machine. Margaret started by building her Customer Offer Machine. Gradually, she watched her Ideal Prospects "get" what she was doing. They started to understand and appreciate there was a rhythm to when she offered classes and how many. Then Margaret stepped into her Customer Marketing Machine and finally her Customer Sales Machine. Her Ideal Customers were able to begin Class #1 and then experience little-to-no delay in starting Class #2. Margaret's Ideal Customers started to buy more classes from her because they fit their schedules, and they knew when they were happening. This is the Customer Machine Margaret built with us to attract the 46,000 followers on Facebook and 16,000 people in her very warm database. Oh, and she's making more money now, too. Way more money (*Oh, more than that*).

BUILD YOUR CUSTOMER MARKETING MACHINE

Coaches' Question: What is your main strategy for attracting new customers for your business? What made you select this strategy?

*If you're like many of our coaching clients, you will answer this question with a laundry list of activities. You're busy but not productive because you don't really have a consistent method or strategy for generating customers. Often, our Ideal Customers tell us they get new customers by the method they feel most comfortable with and competent in using, sometimes one they've used for years. And sometimes that old chestnut of a system isn't working too well. Shift your focus. You **must** choose your customer generating strategy based on how, where and when your Ideal Customer makes their buying decisions. These are steps to building your Customer Machine.*

The more your Ideal Customers become exposed to your business, the more likely they are to follow it. That's why you must uncover **where** your Ideal Customers spend most of their time, both online and offline. Then your job necessitates persistent interaction with them in those arenas, rather than in all those other, random places all the alleged "experts" told you work...though they don't know one single thing about your business.

Before you can grab your Ideal Customer's attention, you must know where to find them.

We're about to introduce you to Customer Machines created based on how, where and when your Ideal Customer makes their buying decisions... and have been proven to actually work to attract Ideal Customers, proven because this is how the highly successful businesses in these industries to do it and what we've developed and repeatedly confirmed through our own work with our Ideal Customers. Why reinvent the wheel, when you can use the round orb proven by others?

One word of caution: you're highly likely to fit into one of the industry Customer Machines we're

YOUR CUSTOMER GENERATION STRATEGY IS BASED ON HOW, WHERE AND WHEN YOUR IDEAL CUSTOMER MAKES THEIR BUYING DECISIONS.

about to show you even if the occupation at the top of the Customer Machine isn't your occupation. Don't get hung up on the title. Search for the Customer Machine nearest to how your industry and you operate.

THE COACH/CONSULTANT CUSTOMER MARKETING MACHINE

You could be a business coach, leadership coach, personal trainer, transitions coach, spiritual coach or dog trainer. Whatever your avenue of specialty, you're a coach and this Customer Machine powers coaching businesses like yours.

No matter the industry for which you consult—manufacturing, software development, router development, cell phone applications, management and so on—you've found your Customer Machine right here.

Just so you have a distinction between these two different yet aligned business models, we look at them this way. A coach leads the Ideal Customer towards the answers they seek which usually exist within them. Consultants often are hired to do the work, to dig in and roll up their sleeves to make something happen. Each delivers a different service in similar ways. So their Customer Marketing Machines are similar, too.

The proven Customer Marketing Machine for these types of services are built with these components:

- **Affiliations** with other businesses who currently work with your Ideal Customer yet don't compete with what you offer

- **LinkedIn** as your social media platform of choice because your Ideal Customers are there

- **Facebook** to offer challenges for followers to complete and report on their results

- **Webinars** to engage new Ideal Prospects

- **Speaking** engagements

Coaches' Question: How much time have you spent digging for new customers? How much time each week do you dedicate to marketing and selling new Ideal Customers? If you don't know the answer, start tracking.

Keep a piece of paper where you work. As you perform marketing functions, write down the effort and how much time you spent on it. Do the same for the time you dedicate to selling. Keep the paper with you for two weeks. What do your results look like?

If they are a bit anemic, perhaps you've found the reason your business isn't growing as you'd like.

Don't be afraid of affiliations as a Customer Marketing Machine component. Affiliations have a double payoff…they make attracting Ideal Prospects easier for you, and they serve your Ideal Customer better than you might be able to do alone.

Let's begin with creating **affiliations**, a magnificent way to build your database and increase your Ideal Prospects, particularly if you're just starting your business. If you've been in business for years, affiliations give your results a booster shot in the arm.

In the kind of affiliations we're talking about, you team up temporarily with another company, probably through a contract that lays out what you plan to do together. You're not starting a new business together; we're talking about marketing affiliations, not legal partnerships. In marketing-style affiliations, you're going to do certain work and your partner will do other, complementary work to create new revenues for each of you.

An effective affiliation creates a win-win for both parties. Otherwise, why would you or your prospective partner work together? Valuable affiliations can follow several models: the affiliate introduces you to your Ideal Customer who they already work with; they agree to introduce you into their database through emails or a free webinar; they introduce you to their database and you introduce them to yours; or you provide them with discount coupons or freebies they can offer to their customers.

When you consider what makes a good affiliation partner, you're looking for:

- An established business

- That already has customers

- Who perfectly fits the profile of your Ideal Customer

- And what that business does complements, not competes, with yours

Working with such an affiliation partner enables you to:

- Gain access to lots of new Ideal Prospects right away without searching for them one or two at a time

- Laser focus your dollars or efforts in the most fertile places

- Make money by winning new business

That's your WIN. What is the WIN for the other business? They:

- Endear and embed themselves more solidly with their existing customers by offering them the "next" thing they need through another source without having to create it themselves

- Reduce or eliminate competition from grabbing their customers (the more you buy from one source, the less likely you are to leave)

- Make some money for doing nothing more than marketing to their customers; they don't have to create a new product or service or create any back-office support such as billing or customer service; it's almost all gravy.

The right affiliation partnership jumpstarts growth.

AH HA MOMENT ⚡: STEPHANIE

Stephanie runs an exercise boot camp and wanted to grow her business. She poked around and realized at least two other business owners in the area served her Ideal Customer, yet they didn't compete with her. They had health and nutrition businesses, an ideal complement to Stephanie's kick-butt boot camp.

She approached the two owners to discuss how they might "share" their customers. After some appropriate due diligence, the three decided to test working together. They chose to start by holding an open house and invite all their customers to a complimentary evening Wellness Camp. The night of the party, the office flowed with customers from all three businesses. Each had a display area showcasing their particular wellness expertise, and how it addressed the problem the guest had. They introduced themselves and their business. They walked the crowd through a brief exercise so the guests could experience their Super Power, not just hear or read about it. They provided material about their services and made a special, extraordinary offer.

The result: Stephanie doubled her clientele in only 90 days. Customers of the other two businesses found Stephanie. Plus, the other two business owners attracted new customers, too.

Win-win-win.

An affiliation grew three businesses through one event.

That might have been an easy example of a successful affiliation. Let's look at a business that's bigger and more sophisticated (no offense, Stephanie).

AH HA MOMENT ⚡: EDWARD

Edward leads a boutique Engineering Firm as its CEO. We were visiting him to work with he and his team on some marketing issues. He invited Chris in and closed his door. He turned slowly and sheepishly shared, "The scariest part of this job is the lack of control I have over the prospects who come through the door." Chris responded, "I thought all your prospects came through your contacts in the venture capital community and serial inventors?"

"Exactly," he replied, "and I never know for certain how many prospects will come in. It feels so arbitrary. Sometimes we have quite a few; other times we have no one. I lose sleep, and I am driving my wife crazy."

Edward had no Customer Machine. He knew his Ideal Customers came through others. He had built loose affiliations with people and other associated businesses. But he had never really sat down to fully develop the relationships, to create stronger ties. In the back of his mind, he knew who had his Ideal Customer, who he could work, who his best affiliation candidates were or what happened once his loose affiliation partner sent him an ideal Prospect. All of that was in his head which meant it's not part of a Customer Machine. Only Edward knew. He never thought about creating an *active* affiliation machine, sitting down with his best, complementary affiliation partners to craft a relationship where both parties won.

You know what we did. I know you can see it coming. We worked with Edward to create his Affiliation Customer Machine. We worked with his team to create and guide their implementation of a Customer Machine for Ideal Prospect generation founded on the affiliation partnership. We systemized his process, rejiggered their sales system, created new customer-centered messaging, developed a warm Ideal Prospect communication process using LinkedIn and dropped in a Google SEO strategy. His Customer Machine was built to enhance his affiliation opportunities and to reward his partners for their efforts. Win-win. As a result, Edward increased his revenue **by $300,000 in one year**.

COACHING EXERCISE 18: *Affiliation Creation*

1. What industry already has your Ideal Customer, doesn't compete with what you do? List them all.

_____

_____

_____

_____

2. Who in those industries operates geographically close to you and you could reach out to them to explore an mutually beneficial affiliation?

_____

_____

_____

_____

3. What's in it for you to affiliate with them?

_____

_____

_____

_____

4. List all the things that are in it for the affiliation partner to create a mutually beneficial relationship with you?

_____

_____

_____

_____

• **Sales Sidebar**

We haven't talked sales with you in a bit. One strategy we have used successfully with our Ideal Customers is to create a series of **LinkedIn** posts that function like an Email campaign. In this strategy, our Ideal Customer publishes a series of six posts over a 10-day period. The campaign aim creates a high level of visibility within a short period of time.

The campaign is designed following an adaptation of the 50/30/20 rule used by financial planners and was first brought to our attention by our Ideal Customer and social media expert, Cheri Martin. In this approach, campaign content is divided as follows:

50%—General Content: Half of your posts should not be related to sales at all, rather about creating engagement and building relationships. These posts include things like jokes or cartoons related to your industry, funny memes, inspirational quotes, short surveys or running contest to keep the momentum going. (3 posts)

30%—Educational Content: These posts focus on news, tips and solutions relevant to your Ideal Customer. You're demonstrating your expertise and positioning yourself as an influencer. The posts include a mix of your own original content and trending information from other sources. An excerpt from a blog post that links back to your website can be used in these posts. (2 posts)

20%—Sales Content: The last post specifically emphasizes your sales offer. For LinkedIn, this should be a "soft-sell" approach, perhaps one cloaked in humor or gentle persuasion.

Once you have mastered this strategy, you can use it over and over. Depending upon the number of contacts you have on LinkedIn, you can run the same campaign multiple times, as the platform limits the number of messages you can send each day. This strategy is essentially a mini-system connecting with your Ideal Prospects more easily, simply and profitably.

One other component of The Coach/Consultant Customer Marketing Machine transpires on Facebook. Sure, having a personal page you use to connect for business purposes, coupled with a business page gives you a foundation for attracting new Ideal Prospects. But what's the level of engagement? Have you attracted many followers? Do they comment when you post? Do you post...regularly?

If your Facebook presence and engagement is a bit blah, boost participation, comments and interaction by offering **challenges** as a routine part of your marketing there. A challenge is...well...just that. Your asking your followers to step up to a task or a contest you pose. A challenge you present to your followers could be to pick something they want to accomplish within seven days. Have them write it down and commit to that goal here on your Facebook page. Then every day for seven days you give them a small task or ask a question to not only keep them engaged but also to move them towards the goal. On the seventh day everyone reports in. How did they do? What insights can you offer about the results they achieved as some will hit their goal and others will miss.

You can build you followers by asking people to share your challenge with others who would be interested by posting the link on their own Facebook page.

A challenge...a challenge right for your Ideal Prospects...boosts followers and follower participation. Your perceived expertise to solve their problem is on display for all to see. Their desire to lean on you for help surges. They become more open to your offer, a small offer (free or for a small fee) made through a link to a landing page belonging to you (rather than Facebook) for which they must opt-in, meaning share their name and email address to receive your offer.

The importance of this last step should not be missed...if your

YOUR FACEBOOK
FOLLOWERS DO
NOT BELONG
TO YOU; THEY
BELONG TO
FACEBOOK!

interaction with your Facebook followers only happens on Facebook, *those are people who belong to Facebook.* They are registered users with Facebook, not you. You might be "friends," you might exchange frequent posts, you might watch them participate in all your challenges. But until they follow you off Facebook and sign-up for something you offer, exchanging their information for your offer, they don't belong to you!

Try a challenge on Facebook. Your results might take a bit of time to build. Your followers will be new to the concept, perhaps, or a challenge coming from you. Over time, you'll watch interaction increase and their willingness to grab your offer multiply.

COACHING EXERCISE 19: *Facebook Challenge*

1. Remember what your Ideal Customer's problem is that you identified in **Part Two: Think Like Your Customer**. List four challenges you could offer on Facebook to create greater engagement with your business followers.

_____

_____

_____

_____

2. Choose one of the challenges you identified above. Map out how it could unfold over seven days. What would you have them do on each of the seven days to reach the end goal?

_____

_____

_____

_____

3. How will you provide support each day to encourage them to continue on the challenge to reach their goal?

_____

_____

_____

_____

_____

Don't worry. *We haven't forgotten to share with you how to create the other components of your Coaching/Consultant Customer Marketing Machine.* **You'll find more conversation below as they are also components in other types of Customer Marketing Machines.**

THE CARE MANAGER/HOME CARE CUSTOMER MARKETING MACHINE

Care managers create and oversee the delivery of a plan of care for seniors. The senior may live at home, in independent living apartments, assisted living facilities or a nursing home. The care manager's role is to work with the family and elder to determine what type of medical and personal care the elder requires now. They work to adjust the plan as the elder's capabilities change. They aid the family and elder in navigating the complexities of the medical maze.

Home care specialists place trained, caring individuals in the home or facility with the elder to make sure they are safe, provide companionship and assist with their activities of daily living.

While similar, each delivers a different service to the elder and their family. If you are a care manager or home care business owner or your business model resembles those businesses, we're about to hand you your Customer Marketing Machine.

The proven Customer Marketing Machine for these types of services clearly indicates:

• An active **referral** system creates the most Ideal Prospects

- Coupled with a **search engine optimization (SEO)** strategy to bring more Ideal Prospects to the website and

- **Content-forward videos** for visitors to view and appreciate that the company understands the problem they want solved (the one the family and elder wants solved)

- **Public speaking events** where referral partners are likely to attend

- With a small dash of **social media**, likely Facebook, supports this machine

The power of **referrals** cannot be denied in any industry. Whenever we teach a marketing workshop, we ask, "How many of you receive some of your business from referrals?" Every hand in the room goes up. Then we ask a kicker. "How many of you get *all* your business from referrals?" Stunningly, most hands stay up. Then the last question…"How many of you actively encourage referrals rather than simply let them happen to you…or not?" A sea of hands descends.

> *Coaches' Question: How much time have you spent systematically seeking and managing referrals for your business? You might be surprised to discover while many of our customers say they receive a hefty percentage of their business from referrals, most do not have a systematic way to ask for and capture referrals and then develop them into an on-going source of Ideal Prospects.*
>
> *What about you? What are you doing to actively cultivate referrals? How much time do you dedicate to developing an active referral system and executing it? If not, you're missing out on a goldmine.*

An Ideal Prospect who arrives in your world by referral already knows plenty about you, how fully you understand the problem they have and how beautifully you enable it to go away. They initially come to you with some level of trust built in because their friend or colleague as sworn to your Super Powers. You don't have to spend a lot of time explaining or getting them "up to speed." They are predisposed to you. In the mind of the person referred, you already have "expert" status, preeminence—a very valuable place to begin a relationship. You can focus faster on connecting with the referral to determine their wants, rather than having to establish your credibility.

Customers who come to you by referral already lean toward purchase. They've heard your praises sung. They connect with the outcome of working with you...the outcome for which they've been searching. Plus, they were interested enough to make the time to contact you or take your call.

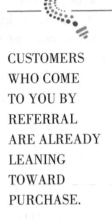

CUSTOMERS WHO COME TO YOU BY REFERRAL ARE ALREADY LEANING TOWARD PURCHASE.

Asking for and encouraging referrals moves you much farther and faster, than waiting for the planets to align and drop them from the sky into your lap. Referrals happen because we humans like to help others. We humans become a hero. Heros rescue people from troubled places. When we refer, we attain hero status (in our eyes certainly and maybe our friend's or colleague's) because we've rescued someone from a dilemma. When you've a customer who had a wonderful experience, they know and trust you. They often want the opportunity to help someone else experience the same benefits they felt.

Once a friend or colleague has shared your name as the champion of that problem, the Ideal Prospect usually follows the same next step to check you out. The friend praises your company and shares how great it is. They heartily recommend they call you, too. They provide your company's name. Before the Ideal Prospect picks up the phone to call or opens their computer to send an email, they'll head over to your website to size up your business. Do you understand my problem? What's the outcome of working with you? And who, exactly are you?

Using **search engine optimization (SEO)** strategies and techniques build the perceived value of your business in the eyes of the visitor and in the spiders of search engines like Google, Yahoo (does anyone remember its new name?) and Explorer. SEO enables your Ideal Prospects to find you faster, whether they have your exact business name written down accurately, or the referring friend really messed up your website address (URL).

Lots of books have been written about SEO. We're not going to go into those details here. If this Customer Marketing Machine aligns with your business...most of your business comes or should come from referrals... then SEO will be an important part of your Customer Marketing Machine.

When the referred individual comes to your website, share some meaningful content. Video content delivers a highly effective method to do that as you can convey quickly you "get" their problem, have the outcome they so desire and have done it for hundreds of people before them…all in under two minutes, the ideal amount of time for busy, impatient visitors.

Video content reigns supreme in popularity as a marketing tool right now. Using video you become both more personable and accessible to your Ideal Customer. Creating an audio and visual presence allows you to enter your Ideal Customer's consciousness through two sensory channels, doubling your opportunity to be remembered. Video on your landing page (your one-page request to do one something and get one something) increases your ability to gain a new Ideal Prospect by 80 percent, according to *EyeWideDigital,* as the visitor is more likely to grab the free offer for information. In this day of smart phones, many people access websites, landing pages and social media through their cellular devices, making long written content difficult to consume. Video relieves this problem.

HAVING A VIDEO ON YOUR LANDING PAGE CAN INCREASE YOUR CONVERSION RATE BY 80%, ACCORDING TO *EYEWIDEDIGITAL.*

You may choose to post your pre-recorded videos on platforms such as You Tube, Facebook or Vimeo or on your own platform such as your website or landing page. Live video can be streamed online through Facebook Live or Zoom. Live videos are generally shorter in duration as your Ideal Customer's attention span isn't what it used to be. Your delivery with live video affords more informal style than pre-recorded videos. Videos may be professionally produced and edited or recorded using your cell phone. If you choose to use your cell, make sure your lighting is good and your audio quality strong. Keep background visuals and noise subdued so you are the center of attention.

Consider these points when creating your video content:

- More and more customers prefer video content to written content; live video can be recorded and repurposed, making it very versatile

- Short, single-topic videos are highly engaging for consumers

- For short live videos, content quality is highly important with production quality less important

- Spontaneous live video is becoming more accepted even in business-to-business marketing

- Video supports the trend toward story-based marketing

- Video must be tailored to the specific platform on which it is published

- Video can yield a high return on investment (ROI) in terms of both time and money

- Video can be used at any stage of your marketing and sales process though it is easier to measure ROI at later stages closer to an actual sale

Social media also plays a small role in the Care Manager and Home Care Customer Marketing Machine. These companies can use a company **Facebook page** to share changes in elder care trends, issues they are seeing increase, post news stories of interest and ask questions of their followers. The families and perhaps the elders can leave comments, too, creating a great public space for dialog. Social media doesn't move the Ideal Prospect needle like a good, active referral machine will for Care Managers and Home Care companies...and you if your business model resembles theirs. Its purpose supports communication and showcases the company's knowledge and expertise in an easily accessible manner.

If your business resembles that of Care Managers or Home Care companies, your Customer Marketing Machine comprises an active referral system, SEO, video content and a dash of social media. Anything else might improve your results a tad, but perhaps not enough to warrant the extra effort and cost.

> *Coaches' Question: How much time do you spend on social media sites for your buiness? What is your strategy for using these sites? And are you achieving the results you want? Or has it been a rather large waste of time? If social media is a key component of your Customr Machine, make sure your strategy delivers.*

AH HA MOMENT ⚡ : CARE MANAGERS

In the Care Management industry, businesses focus on keeping seniors in their home, lowering acuity (avoiding high-end, high-cost care) and getting all the elder's medical, health and care providers working together on therapies, medicines and care. Our clients in the Care Management field typically receive 10 or so inquiries every week from potential customers, Ideal Prospects.

On average, the Care Managers enroll three of the 10. Often, no one tracks who sent the 10 to them nor records the source for future use. The referral source might have been shared during the call, but it wasn't documented. Therefore, referrals happen randomly, rather than proactively.

We work with our Care Management companies to create an active referral system as the primary driver of their Customer Machine. Now when someone calls the person receiving the call asks how they found out about the company. That person then puts the name of the referral source in a software system. They can then begin to track their best referral sources. They reach out to those sources and ask for a meeting, maybe over a cup of coffee. They thank them for the best and share whatever they are allowed by law to share about the outcome of the elder. They then share the very best Ideal Customer they seek, emphasis the problem they solve, not only for the family and their elder, but also the referring party. They help them, too! And, they ask a simple question, "What other clients might you have who fit this profile and have a similar problem? How can we help you serve these clients better?"

AH HA MOMENT : CYNTHIA

Cynthia had not taken a vacation in years. Her team was over-worked, and she was beginning to feel as though she was "stuck" with her business. Cynthia didn't need to be stuck as there was an easily identifiable Customer Machine to make her world a better, happier, less "stuck" place.

We coached Cynthia to put the following Customer Machine in place:

1. An active referral strategy that included a letter campaign, in-person visits and phone calls to her best candidates for referrals

2. A new SEO strategy to increase online visibility

3. Content creation for her website and online platforms, including videos

4. A structured plan for expansion to other zip codes

5. An editorial calendar for marketing activities that was useable every year

6. Increased social media presence, especially on Facebook

7. Regular local speaking engagements—becoming the known expert in Care Management

8. A new hiring system that put the right people in the right positions

9. A revised revenue model that maximized ROI

Cynthia's new Customer Machine is so successful she scheduled a vacation with confidence and took it! She knew she had the right person in place to keep the business running while she was away. Cynthia now has a succession plan to sell her business and retire within the next five years.

While you'll see a lot of elements to Cynthia's Customer Marketing Machine, the active referral system tipped her business forward mightily.

Does your business resemble that of a Care Manager or Home Care company? If so, look above. You now have your Customer Marketing Machine!

THE PROFESSIONAL SERVICES CUSTOMER MARKETING MACHINE

Our definition of professional services includes attorneys, CPAs, Certified Financial Planners, dentists, chiropractors and insurance agents, really those occupations in the services sector of the economy requiring special training and/or licensing. The services provided revolve around attention, advice, access or experience. In other words, these professions are not manufacturing goods or creating raw materials for manufacturing.

Their Customer Marketing Machines closely resemble each other, so close let's call it a bump.

The proven Customer Marketing Machine for these types of services clearly builds from:

- **Networking**

- The same active **referral** strategy we discussed above

- **Speaking** engagements and

- **Affiliations** with other professionals who already have your Ideal Customer, yet do not compete with you

Again, these businesses…and you if this resembles your business model or industry…could toss in a small dash of social media, LinkedIn in this case, to support the awareness and development of their brand.

Networking creates a practice of intentionally forming relationships for mutual benefit. Successful networkers make a plan, commit to it and execute it consistently. You choose your networking events and times based on the likelihood your Ideal Customer participates in the association and its events.

Networking provides far more than sharing a few lukewarm appetizers, a glass of house wine and an opportunity to swap business cards with other people. You can engage in networking at events, activities and locations not specifically designed for business networking.

For example, if your Ideal Customer looks like a busy career woman with young kids who is feeling overcommitted and overwhelmed by all the professional and family jobs she's required to do, where might you find her? On the sidelines at her kid's soccer game, at an professional association meeting or at a brown bag lunch event at her company. If she, your Ideal Customer, can be found in these events, you should be at those events. Perhaps you sponsor the soccer team, join the professional association and participate or sign up to be one of the sponsors of the brown bag lunch. Your goal is to meet people, ask interesting, problem-identifying questions and share how you take the problem away. Ask if you can reach out to them at another time. Leave with their contact information and, ideally, with a dates and time set for that next conversation.

Coaches' Question: When you leave a networking event have you given out your business cards or have you gathered business cards? If you're handing out your cards to prospective Ideal Prospects, that's nice. If, however, you aren't getting their business cards, you've just handed over the responsibility of follow-up to the Ideal Prospect. Who's more likely to follow up, the prospect or you?

If you came home from a networking event with every business card you left with, we'd be fine with that as long as you also came home with the cards of people you met with whom you'll follow up. With cards in your hand, you're in charge of the next step of the budding relationship rather than them. Then follow up. Don't let the business cards stack up on your desk without reaching out. After all, isn't that why you went to the event? To find new Ideal Prospects?

Good networkers ask cause-and-effect questions and then listen. Think of your networking conversations as market research where you can uncover more about the wants, challenges and preferences of your potential Ideal Prospects.

Networking usually occurs in face-to-face settings. They can also be done electronically. Facebook offers an interesting method for electronic interaction, as does LinkedIn. Choose where you will network based on what you know about your Ideal Customer. Join and network in groups where you will find your potential Ideal Prospect or people who can connect you with your potential Ideal Prospect.

Maximize your investment in networking by following these recommendations:

THINK OF YOUR NETWORKING CONVERSATIONS AS MARKET RESEARCH WHERE YOU CAN DISCOVER MORE ABOUT THE WANTS, CHALLENGES, AND PREFERENCES OF YOUR POTENTIAL IDEAL PROSPECTS.

- Focus on connection, rather than on self-promotion…nobody likes the pushy, self-centered person at a networking event

- Listen more than you speak…take notes on their business card to aid your memory when you're back in your office

- Write down five objectives you want to achieve during and after the event; check your list during the event to note progress and what you still must put into action; stay on your objectives when you're back in your office…that way the event produces a Return on Your Investment (ROI) when you achieve your objectives

CHOOSE WHERE
TO NETWORK
BASED ON WHAT
YOU KNOW
ABOUT YOUR
CUSTOMER.

- Research before arriving so you know the types of people you are likely to meet at a specific event… then you're prepared and on your toes to create a positive event for your business

- Be prepared to describe concisely who you are and what you do; you created your Elevated Ingredients in **Part Three: Act Like Your Customer**; use it

- Follow-up, follow-up, follow-up

COACHING EXERCISE 20: Networking

1. List the types of networking events you attend most frequently. Does your Ideal Customer participate in these events? Or do you attend for other reasons?

_____

_____

_____

_____

_____

2. For each type of activity, give a score between 1 and 5, with 1 being Not Very Successful in creating Ideal Prospects and 5 being Extremely Successful.

_____

_____

_____

_____

_____

3. Place the list of activities in the order of how much time you spend on each one. List the one you spend the most time at the top and work down.

_____

_____

_____

_____

_____

4. Look at the lists in Questions 2 and Does your time expenditure match the success score for each activity? If not, what would you adjust?

_____

_____

_____

_____

_____

5. List at least 5 places or groups you believe offer good networking opportunities for your business because your Ideal Customers attend. How many are you networking in now? Is there anything you can do (or should do) to step up your networking game?

_____

_____

_____

_____

_____

Speaking engagements seems to be greatly underused as a Customer Machine component, and we're not surprised. Did just reading the words "public speaking" give you a frightening chill? Public speaking brings out the "gulp" in most people, and they say many people fear public speaking more than they fear death! You can relate, can't you? If so, we want to encourage you to conquer this fear, so you grab opportunities others leave behind and put you face-to-face with your Ideal Customers.

Speaking boosts your business and should become a more frequent part of your Customer Machine, particularly if you offer attention, advice, access or experience services:

1. Speaking maximizes efficiency...because it allows you to reach many people at the same time

2. Speaking positions you as an expert in your chosen field; the fact you are in front of the room automatically signals you have something important to share...shortcutting the attendee's journey to trust

3. Speaking provides a captive audience of Ideal Customers; when you stand at the front of the room or on a stage, you have little competition for your audience's attention versus all the distractions they have when you're presenting online...so your message has a substantial opportunity to sink in and stick

4. Speaking invites follow-up and continued contact; when you effectively engage your audience, you can give them a call-to-action (sign up for a complimentary exploratory conversation, buy your book, go home with your free e-book or business tip, for example) they will be eager to reach out to you to learn more and might even buy the thing you offer on the spot...connecting you directly and effectively to your Ideal Customer to build trust fast and engage sooner.

When you're speaking, you're speaking to begin your sales process rather than educate the audience on their problem and how you solve it. You'll speak about only the "what" and "why" of the problem. What their problem is. Why they have this problem. What the outcome of working with you is. Why you're their finest choice to solve their problem.

Your conversation is never about "how"...how you solve their problem.

They pay you for your "how." They pay you for your solution. If you hand over the solution to the problem while you're speaking, what do they need you for? Even if you've only shared a sliver of the solution your audience will leave believing they have enough, at least for now. Their buying motivator has been satisfied because you've handed over a free solution.

Think and act "what" and "why" not "how."

THINK AND ACT "WHAT" AND "WHY" NOT "HOW."

COACHING EXERCISE 21: Speaking Engagements

1. List all the topics you can speak about and your Ideal Customer wants to know about?

_____

_____

_____

_____

_____

2. As you prepare your public conversation, "what" is the problem you'll address?

_____

_____

_____

_____

_____

3. What is the "why" they have the problem you'll discuss?

_____

_____

_____

_____

4. What is the "what is the outcome of working with you" you'll share?

_____

_____

_____

_____

_____

5. Why should they work with you? List all the reasons.

_____

_____

_____

_____

_____

_____

AH HA MOMENT ⚡: MARTHA AND CHRIS

Not all Ah Ha Moments stroll down the path as great successes. Sometimes Ah Ha Moments arrive on a plate for eating crow.

In early 2009 we ran the ultimate…THE ULTIMATE…promotion for one of our new services. We worked closely with the 1,500 Chambers of Commerce in California. We knew…KNEW…we had a spectacular program for them to offer to their small business owners. The program would increase participation in the Chamber by its members, one of the issues plaguing Chambers, and substantial revenue would come to them as an affiliation fee for permitting us to offer the program to its members. For Chamber members, the program would show them how to boost their business without spending a new fortune or adding more costly team to their business. For us, the revenue from sales we forecasted would double the best results we'd ever attained. This program was a winner for everyone.

The Chambers promoted the program. We supported their promotion with emails and literature. Chris attended Chamber events to tell the members about the new program coming that would boost their business without additional spending or team.

The needle barely moved. Members didn't sign up for the program.

But why? We knew it was perfect. The Chamber leaders loved it. Its Members didn't seem to care.

What we have here is the perfect example of building something you believe someone wants without asking them. Our fatal mistake was we never ran the idea for the program by the people we believed wanted it. If we had, we would have made substantial changes in the program. But we didn't.

After many hours of working and promoting the new program and knocking on many Chamber doors, we realized the offering was NOT what the Chamber members wanted, and they were simply not going to buy it.

We had built the wrong Customer Machine.

Chris took it hard, as a true failure. After much wringing of hands and soul searching, we realized although the program did not generate the impact we had planned on, it brought about many other unplanned, unforeseen gems. We regrouped. We repackaged the offering and launched the program in a new way, a way that all our questions, poking and prodding indicated someone other than Chamber members wanted.

We turned failure into triumph…but only after much head hanging, second guessing and spent money. We think of this now as our own little moment of GRIT.

Does your business resemble that of a Professional Services company? If so, there's your Customer Marketing Machine.

OFFICE-BASED SERVICES BUSINESS
CUSTOMER MARKETING MACHINE

When you take you poochie to the veterinarian, finally walk into the dentist's office, have your hair restyled or decide its time the chiropractor worked the kink out of your back, you've stepped into an office-based services business. You must go into their office to receive their services, unlike how you interact with the professional services businesses discussed above.

Guess what? Their Customer Marketing Machines closely resemble each other. And their Customer Marketing Machine might be your Customer Marketing Machine if your business resembles an office-based services business.

The proven Customer Marketing Machine for these types of services builds on:

- An active on-line **social proof** and **reviews**

- **Social media**

- **Reengaging former customers**

- Actively maintaining their **website**

The world today loves to see **social proof** of your trustworthiness and ability to solve your Ideal Customer's problem. Your Ideal Customer moves very cautiously these days and rightly so. The Internet puts both evil and evil geniuses in the palm of your Ideal Customer's hands. Which one are you? Building your independent social proof of your extraordinary talents at taking away a problem enables you to use the Internet for its evil genius good.

Social proof provides the world with powerful words from your Ideal Customer about what their experience with you was. You've likely read Yelp reviews, customer comments on Google and Amazon customer comments before you decided to buy a product or service. Just the other day Martha's family made a decision to pass on an oral surgeon based on poor reviews online. When she called his office to cancel the appointment, they asked the reason for the cancellation. She shared honestly. Poor online reviews. The receptionist didn't seem to care.

You should care.

Social proof creates one of the seven most powerful ways to influence, according to Robert B. Cialdini in his seminal work, *Influence: The Psychology of Persuasion*. Social proof provides an enormous boost to "yes." If 52 or 520 people give you four- and five-star ratings online, what do you think that will do to the next reader? You'll look certifiably awesome.

The more frequent the positive online reviews the more significant your awesomeness becomes. Reviews provide a significant boost especially for local searches. Independent review sites such as Yelp and Google Business provide customers with an opportunity to post their opinion about your business. Reviews on these sites work in the same way testimonials on your website do, providing social proof you can be trusted and deliver positive results. Think of online reviews as a risk-reduction strategy for your Ideal Customer.

ONLINE REVIEWS PROVIDE SOCIAL PROOF YOU CAN BE TRUSTED AND DELIVER POSITIVE RESULTS.

Put this url into your browser: https://www.yelp.com/biz/cetana-salon-san-francisco

Cetana Salon is owned by Martha's hair stylist from her decades in the San Francisco area. What you'll see is pages and pages of four- and five-star reviews. In the rare instance a lower review pops up, Jay, the business manager, leaves a supporting and sometimes apologetic comment. He'll leave "thank yous" for many of the wonderful reviews, too.

If you lived or were visiting San Francisco and had the urge for a haircut or new styling, Cetana would impress. Their social proof vibrates with awesomeness. The awesomeness leads to rapid "yes." And "yes" leads to a very booked group of stylists.

How does Cetana Salon do this? How do they muster so many amazing reviews?

First, they do it through amazing services, creating very beautiful and handsome customers. They take photos of the new look using the clients cell phone (also their cameras for marketing purposes). This gives the client a shot they can post on their own Facebook or Instagram account to show off their beautiful/handsome moment.

And then they ask for a review. As you can easily see, their clients rush home and gush praises for Cetana Salon.

Cetana's customers are highly motivated to offer a review. Cetana makes it easy for the client by taking a photo and asking for the review.

If you have an office-based services business or a business close to this model, are you actively encouraging reviews, social proof? Where is your Ideal Customer likely to look for online reviews of your business? Encourage your Ideal Customers to post your review there first. Please make sure the information in your listing matches the information on your website and on Google Pages. Otherwise, your reviews may not show up in a search. Staple a review request on your Ideal Customer's bill when they check out. If you feel your Ideal Customer isn't completely savvy with posting a review, provide a brief set of instructions to walk them through the process on your preferred site.

The timing of your ask is critical. Your Ideal Customer is most likely to take time to post a positive review when they are flooded with happy feelings about working with you. You've solved their problem or enhanced their life. Waiting to ask as their memory and enthusiasm fades doesn't maximize the moment.

Be sure to thank customers for positive reviews and to respond respectfully and appropriately to negative ones. Being responsive to customer feedback provides a boost to your credibility.

YOUR FORMER CUSTOMERS AREN'T DEAD. THEY'RE JUST SLEEPING, WAITING TO HEAR FROM YOU AGAIN.

Office-based Service Providers sit on another goldmine that will motor their Customer Marketing Machine to stunning results...**reengaging former customers**. They are the prize in the Cracker Jack box when you reach in and pull it out.

If you've been in business for any length of time, you have former customers. They aren't currently working with you. Perhaps they haven't engaged your services in quite some time. They aren't dead. They're just sleeping, waiting for you to nudge them awake, to hear from you again.

The reason why your former customers offer you such potential and absolutely must be part of your Customer Machine resides in the simple fact you likely haven't solved all their problems. The first work they did with you solved some of the problem. Either a part of the problem lingers because their issue was just too big to heal with one step, or a new problem has risen up or...you know what...they might be ready for that vitamin we talked about in **Part Two: Think Like Your Customer**. Any way you look at it, there's more work to be done with your former customers.

If you believe your former customers will just call you when they are ready, please come back to reality. They might have every intention of calling. Then ten thousand other things derail their best intentions. They aren't calling you. Probably. Your role in their life means you're the leader, you're the problem solver. Pick up the phone and reconnect.

In our best-selling book, *Customers Are The Answer to Everything*, we dug into a detailed discussion on how to revive your dead, as we irreverently call it. Grab the book for the full view into this opportunity.

In the meantime, if you're scratching your head about how to begin your reengagement with former customers, here's what we said then. It still applies now.

1. **Set your intention and have a plan.** Calling up a former customer you haven't talked to in months (or years) and pitching them on your latest product will likely sound a bit mercenary. Think of how you would respond to such a call. You risk losing a very good prospect. Focus instead on reestablishing contact with them first. Have a long-range plan that includes the intention of turning them into an active customer again but remember not to become so focused on the goal that you lose touch with nurturing the relationship. And on the other hand, don't spend so much time nurturing the relationship that you forget your goal is to revive them.

2. **Be prepared.** Refresh your knowledge about this person before you pick up the phone to call them. What did they buy from you and when? What was their experience like? What problems did you solve for them? What was their most likely next step based on the work you did with them last? Do you recall anything personal or unique about them (names of their children or spouse, their hobbies or interests)? Set your purpose and course in your mind before you call, e-mail or contact them.

3. **Reestablish yourself as an expert.** Look for opportunities to share your expertise, particularly if they "didn't know you did that." Look for a way to give something back to them and reestablish the benefits of working

with you. Focus on their problem or need. Talk about that and what it would be like to have that problem solved or need delivered. *Do not solve their problem when you talk to them.* If you solve their problem, they don't need to work with you, do they?

4. **Give them something free.** Everyone loves getting something for free. It's a tactic we frequently use in getting new customers but one we forget to use with existing customers. Offer a free e-book, your instructional newsletter, a report, or something of value that will remind them of the benefits of working with you

5. **Express your appreciation.** Take the time to tell them you appreciated working with them and appreciated their business. Give them some love. Most of us suffer from chronic under-appreciation. A genuine expression of gratitude goes a very long way, because it's so rare in the business world. When was the last time someone thanked you for your business? It's been awhile, hasn't it? Yet I'm sure you love it when it does happen. Think of ways to thank your customers. Take a group of them to lunch and ask them to invite their business friends who might need your services. Create customer appreciation and loyalty programs that give special benefits and rewards to your best customers. These are just a few ideas. What are yours?

6. **Ask for a Success Story.** You've probably thought of Success Stories as a way to build your credibility because they're more powerful than simple testimonials. Your instincts on that are right on the money. Now we want you to recognize another power that Success Stories bring: a way to acknowledge and honor your customers. By highlighting a customer with his name, company name or photo and allowing him to share his experience, you honor him as a spokesperson for you and give them a chance to "show off" his own success. While many larger businesses resist participating in Success Stories because they seem more beneficial to you than them, don't give up too easily. If you cast the business as a hero, they get a completely different benefit than they've received from a Success Story before. They get time in the spotlight, can showcase how great their business is, and show how always-current they are keeping their business as an "expert."

AH HA MOMENT ⚡: ROB

When we worked with Rob, he owned a hearing aid store with a database of 3,500 people who bought from him in the past. We asked him how many of his clients buy a second and third hearing aid from him as new technology arrives quickly. His answer was appalling. Very few.

We smelled opportunity. We dug in. "Rob, how often should a person buy a new hearing aid due to improvements in technology?" "Every three years," replied Rob. "Rob," we continued, "about how many former customers in your database have purchased hearing aids over three years ago?" About two-thirds he estimated. Okay, not so bad. Then we poked a little deeper. "Are you using your database to engage the other one third who haven't purchased in at least three years?" Nope. Next question. "How much does a hearing aid cost?" Around $3,000 to $7,000, give or take a few dollars depending on what they require.

Let's do some math here. Rob has one third of his database who haven't bought a hearing aid from him in at least three years. That's 1,166 people. Multiply that times the price of a new hearing aid. 1,166 times $3000 and $7,000.

Rob had $3,498,000-to-$8,162,000 of opportunity undeveloped yet right at his fingertips.

Yes, we know every one of those 1,166 people were not going to buy another hearing aid from Rob. If just a fraction did, Rob would be on easy street (directions, please?).

So we challenged him. Of course, we did. You've got the hang of us by now. "Start making calls to those people, Rob, who already like you and purchased from you in the past," we mandated. He scheduled 17 new appointments in the first week alone. One month into his Customer Marketing Machine, he'd increased revenue in his practice by an additional $79,000! His customers were thrilled to hear from him (no pun intended), and they appreciated the opportunity to upgrade their hearing aid products to ones that served them better.

He had millions sitting in his database, and through one month's effort of reengaging his former customers his increased his revenue by $79,000. In one month, plus his usual sales.

Can you imagine how much business is sitting in *your* entire database of former customers?

··
COACHING EXERCISE 22: Reengaging Former Customers

1. How many former customers do you have? If 10 percent of them returned to do business with you, how much revenue would that deliver, assuming they spend as much as last time? What if 20 percent returned?

_____

_____

_____

_____

2. If ten percent of your former customers returned to work with you again and this time spent ten percent more money with you, how much revenue would that create? If they spent twenty percent more? Yes, I know this is math. It's good for you!

_____

_____

_____

_____

3. If both above happened, what percentage of your yearly revenue target would be achieved, easing the pressure to create new, more expensive prospects?

_____

_____

_____

_____

4. Write your first Success Story:

The Problem:

_____

_____

_____

Your Solution:

_____

_____

_____

The Result:

_____

_____

_____

BUILD YOUR CUSTOMER OFFER MACHINE

As you build your entire Customer Machine, your complete machine may require an offer component. Remember the conversation earlier in this **Part Four** about McDonald's, Burger King and Wendy's? One of the difference in their Customer Machines was their offering: grill-top burgers versus flame-broiled burgers versus a special price bundled offer. Each company differentiates themselves and attracts their particular Ideal Customer by creating an offer/product their Ideal Customer desires. And the offer is built in a machine-like fashion.

Your offers/services are designed to solve your Ideal Customer's problem.

ODDS ARE SEVERAL SERVICE OFFERINGS WILL BE REQUIRED TO TOTALLY OR NEAR-TOTALLY ELIMINATE THE PROBLEM.

So, how do you know what the customer wants? **Part Two: Think Like Your Customer** holds the answer. You can ask them!

Once you know the problem they want to solve, you'll design a product/service to eliminate or reduce the problem. Now, please remember something else we've discussed: while you can probably solve their entire problem with one service, your Ideal Customer likely cannot absorb everything in one service.

Odds are several service offerings will be required to totally or near-eliminate the problem.

• **Sales Sidebar**

We know how to solve your business problems/challenges/issues/dilemmas with one service offering. We also know you would be overwhelmed trying to absorb and implement the entire solution through one service. You'll be overcome, which is not the foundation of who we are (creating easier, simpler and more profitable businesses is who we are). We'll determine the right steps, in phases and march you down the path to your goal at a speed you can handle. You know the expression, "The pack moves as swiftly as its leader." You're the leader of your business. We'll proceed as swiftly as you. Maybe give you a little push now and again to pick up the pace. We're here and want to work with you.

Your offer assembles more than the product or service itself. Your offer includes elements that deliver additional value to your customers, such as availability, convenient delivery, technical support, pricing, special offers, bundling and quality of service. A well-crafted offer sets you apart from your competitors and builds value by meeting your Ideal Customer's wants better than the competition does.

To create an offering, you must understand what is most important to your Ideal Customer and then determine the best way to deliver it. Keep in mind your Ideal Customer cares not a hoot about the *features* of your offer. *They care about the outcome of working with you.* How they change. How they are transformed. That their problem goes away or dissipates.

Customers buy based on what they believe your product or service will do for them.

What will they see, think, feel, have or do as a result of your offer?

When you can clearly demonstrate the outcome, your offer becomes attractive to your Ideal Customer by adding value to their health, wealth, relationships or business.

THE COACH/CONSULTANT CUSTOMER OFFER MACHINE

Coaches, your Ideal Customers might not be ready to meet you, be attracted to you, believe you can solve their problem…and leap into the deep in of the pool by saying "yes" to your 12-month coaching package. That's a very big first commitment. What if they don't like you when they begin working with you? That's probably rolling through their mind as they consider your offer.

Think of your offer as if you're dating. A 12-month coaching program when you've just met feels a bit like asking them to get married. You're moving too fast too soon.

CUSTOMERS BUY BASED ON WHAT THEY BELIEVE YOUR PRODUCT OR SERVICE WILL DO FOR THEM.

Your Customer Offer Machine might look more like this:

- Coaching twice a month for three months

- Then an offer to continue with coaching twice a month for six months

- Perhaps next, your offer is either to re-up for six months or move to a 12-month program

- Finally, a once-a-month program for on-going support and account-ability once they've demonstrated they've rounded the corner on their challenge

Consultants, the dating analogy works for you, too. Your Ideal Customer company might think you are their savior yet still hesitate to make a long-term commitment to you that's hard to get out of if things don't work as either of you believe.

An alternative approach to all-in could make your Customer Offer Machine look like:

- Phase 1: Assessment of the issue

- Phase 2: A plan to solve the problem

- Phase 3: Step 1 of the plan

- Phase 4: Step 2 of the plan

- Etc

You will introduce and outline all Phases in your proposal. Your Ideal Customer could say "yes" to just Phase 1 to create comfort and gain confidence in your ability to work with them. As Phase 1 draws towards completion and you review results with your Ideal Customer, you ask them to commit to Phase 2, and so on. You might find your Ideal Customer is completely willing and able to say "yes" to all Phases. This proposal approach gives them the flexibility to move at their own pace. By the way, we suggest you reduce the overall price of all Phases if they say "yes" to everything up front. It's a great encouragement to close the entire deal!

AH HA MOMENT ⚡: MARTHA AND CHRIS

For many years, we felt a little stumped by our own Idea Customer's journey through our business. It always felt a little random.

One day we sat down to really take a look at the Wide Awake Business Ideal Customer journey. We talked with our CRM (client relationship management) partner, and he gave us two words that changed the way we view our Ideal Customer offer and relationship.

The two magic words are *"then what."* "Then what" do you want your customer to do next? "Then what" do you want them to do after that? And, "then what" do you want them to do if they do not do the first "then what?" It changed our whole paradigm to view our Customer Offer Machine as a series of **connected conversations and offers** leading our Ideal Customer to what they want, coupled with what we know they need. Our business growth went "BOOM" as a result.

We're giving you a behind the scenes look at our own process of connecting the dots in our Customer Offer Machine to show you two things:

1. Even experienced business owners require help to accurately and thoroughly understand their Ideal Customer journey

2. Once you master your Customer Offer Machine and can answer the "then what" question, you open the door to growth

We're here to plot your Ideal Customer journey with you.

THE CARE MANAGER/HOME CARE CUSTOMER OFFER MACHINE

Most Care Management and Home Care companies receive calls weekly from people inquiring about their services. The companies walk through a litany of offerings, sometimes get the name and contact information of the caller, and then leave the responsibility of next-step to the caller. And the caller doesn't call back. About 7 of 10 inquiries amount to no offer accepted or even second call.

If you're a Care Manager, Home Care owner or a business resembling their model, what if your Customer Offer Machine looked like this:

- Offer 1: Elder assessment with no other commitments

- Offer 2: Quarterly or yearly reassessments

- Offer 3: Weekly or monthly care management or in-home care

- Offer 4: On-going care management or in-home care

How many more of those lost seven callers would turn into Ideal Customers? Several of our Care Management and Home Care companies are integrating this Customer Offer Machine right now. Stand by for results!

AH HA MOMENT ⚡ : CARE MANAGERS

In the Care Management industry, businesses focus on keeping seniors in their home, lowering acuity (avoiding high-end, high-cost care) and getting all the care providers working together on therapies, medicines and care. Most of our Care Management Ideal Customers field 10 inquiries weekly from Ideal Prospects. On average, Care Managers enroll three of the 10. What happens to the other seven? They walk away without a care plan or anything tangible. That is without the Care Manager establishing an ongoing relationship with the caller.

What would it be like to create a Customer Offer Machine? What if the Care Manager interviewed the other seven Ideal Prospects and figured out what services the Care Managers could provide in *advance of a crisis?* Maybe a care management plan with follow up review once a year or once a quarter. Or interim calls to help the family or spouse prepare for the future.

Maybe they would feel so comfortable, placing high trust with the Care Management company's service they would say "yes" to other services as the acuity progressed in their own family. Maybe they'd refer a friend or other family member. Without that clear "then what?" system in place, Care Managers will never know how much business they are leaving behind.

THE PROFESSIONAL SERVICES CUSTOMER OFFER MACHINE

As a professional services company, you may only provide services to your clients during a few times of the year. CPAs are swamped from end January through mid-April with small burst of busyness during September and October for late filers. Financial Services experts may only meet their Ideal Customer once a year. And for cryin' out loud, when was the last time your insurance agent called you?

Imagine a shift in how these professional service providers delivered their services. What if they had adjunct, complementary programs to offer? The CPA offered bookkeeping services or entity services. What if the financial planners had programs where you met with them officially and methodically quarterly and before the end of the calendar year so you could adjust your investment for better tax and investment returns. What if your insurance agent actually called you? For anything!

If your business model delivers professional services, you've left so much business on the table our head spins.

What if your Customer Offer Machine looked like this:

- Initial service offering such as taxes, investment review and realignment and car insurance

- Semi-annual or quarterly reviews to discussed and implement better tax strategies based on your situation, investment discussions for adjustments to improve returns against any tax considerations and insurance reviews of all your needs, not just your car

- Concierge services, paid monthly, for on-going access to the CPA and financial planner

A Customer Offer Machine for professional services changes the entire dynamic of how services are delivered and how Ideal Customers enrich their situation through consistent access and reviews. This Machine can utterly transform the relationship you have with your Ideal Customers and accelerate your income exponentially.

THE OFFICE-BASED SERVICES BUSINESS CUSTOMER OFFER MACHINE

When we finally make the time to take our pup to the vet, bring our teeth to the dentist and carry our aching back to the chiropractor, we've found time for a might difficult task. Too many of us postpone these services until we can postpone them no more. Then we pat ourselves on the back for putting the checkmark in the box, and we don't return again until we have another issue.

What if you, who is an office-based service business, made it more compelling and easier for your Ideal Customers to return again and again?

Are you game? If so, your Customer Offer Machine can look like this:

- Initial service offering such as annual pet check-up, teeth cleaning or back adjustment

- A package of complementary services such as ear cleaning (for the pet, not you), teeth whitening and products to keep the body adjusted through the rigors of daily life, with bundled pricing

- A wellness program, sold and pre-scheduled

- Concierge services, paid monthly, for on-going access...maybe even delivered to your home

A Customer Offer Machine for office-based professional services almost guarantees a full schedule of appointments as existing Ideal Customers see the value in using you in more accessible ways.

··························
COACHING EXERCISE 23: Describe Your Offering

1. What is your initial product or service offering to your Ideal Customers to receive an easier "yes" from your Ideal Customer?

_____

_____

_____

_____

_____

2. What could your Customer Offer Machine look like if you created a funnel of services bundled or unbundled to make it easier your Ideal Customer to say "yes" initially and continue to buy from you to completely eliminate their problem?

_____

_____

_____

_____

_____

_____

3. Once your eliminate your Ideal Customer's problem, what could be the "vitamin" service you offer to continue your engagement with them?

_____

_____

_____

_____

_____

> Remember, all these Coaching Exercises are available
> to you, along with special offers on our website:
> wideawakebusiness.com/resources

PART FOUR

BUILD YOUR CUSTOMER SALES MACHINE

Coaches' Question: When you're asked what you do or what your business is, do you answer, "I'm in sales?" What feelings does that answer create for you?

*If you are like most of our Ideal Customers, you don't say you're "in sales." The truth be told, if you're in business, you **must** to be in sales. Very few of our Ideal Customers say they love sales when we begin working with them. In fact, mostly they want to run from sales. Many are afraid they'll come off as pushy or sales-y. So, they may call once. Maybe. Instead, they just keep putting out information about their business hoping sales magically appear. Guess what? They won't!*

Focus first on serving your Ideal Customer better than anyone else. When you do and people experience it, sales...strong sales...naturally follow.

Your Customer Machine now has strong marketing and offer components. You're attracting Ideal Prospects and making offers that appeal and showcase value. But without the sale, so what?

Ideal Customers often get stuck right in the idea of selling. Ugh. Sales. They didn't start their businesses to be salespeople. They started their businesses to deliver the things they love, to share their special talent or skills, to make a difference in the world.

For most of our Ideal Customers, sales is a five-letter word that feels like a four-letter word. Selling doesn't conjure up happy thoughts. They are skittish and resist. They so want to avoid and generally think miserable thoughts about selling.

SELL *FOR* YOUR CUSTOMER, RATHER THAN JUST SELLING *TO* YOUR CUSTOMER.

We can't tell you how often we hear our Ideal Customers say, "I don't want to be sales-y." Our response? If you want to serve your customers, you must sell to your customers. Repeatedly. You build your business by turning your Ideal Customers into raving fans. We like to think of it as selling *for* your customer, rather than selling *to* your customer.

We want you to think of selling this way. Your Ideal Customer has a problem, a headache. You have an aspirin in your pocket. Your aspirin will take away their headache. And just because you're afraid of "selling," you're going to keep the aspirin in your pocket and let them continue to suffer with the headache. Really?? You're nicer than that.

You do a disservice to your customers when you sell them too little, when you sell them more than they need or when you sell them the wrong product. When you don't sell.

AH HA MOMENT ⚡: CHRIS

One day Chris' cleaning crew, aka "all five kids," were ready to clean the house. They came running in with smiles, thrilled beyond words because the vacuum cleaner was broken. They wouldn't be able to do vacuum, *giggle giggle*.

Chris excused them for three hours. In the meantime, she ran off to Sears (an hour and half round trip) to buy a new vacuum cleaner. Returning home, Chris put the cleaning crew back on the job.

Three months go bye. The cleaning crew has been vacuuming up a storm weekly. The next week one of the crew charges upstairs to report, "The vacuum is broken. We won't be able to finish our chores, *giggle giggle*."

Steaming mad at Sears, Chris headed down the hill yet again to fix the problem. The sales person confessed the vacuum she purchased required a filter and bag to be replaced every three months. Eyeing the very same sales associate, Chris cornered him on why he didn't sell her extra filters and bags when she bought the vacuum. "I was trying to save you money and not jeopardize the sale," he offered.

Chris looked dumb-founded. "So, instead you sold me too little of what I required to make the vacuum purchase a delight and force me to make an unnecessary one and a half drive? I have my cleaning crew on hold waiting for the vacuum to be fixed."

The entire journey "cost" Chris over three hours of time, hours of irritation and the undoing of her well-organized crew. Chris took the opportunity to share her frustration with the young sales associate and remind him he sold her too little. How much smarter he would have been to sell her what she must have, not too little or too much, in the first place.

Do you do that to your Ideal Customer? Either not sell them at all or sell them too little because you're terrified of putting your problem-solving and price in front of them?

Your Ideal Customers want an easier, simpler and more effective way to resolve their problem. You want to create an easier, simpler, more profitable business. These two things seem aligned.

CREATE AN EASIER, SIMPLER, MORE PROFITABLE BUSINESS BY SELLING YOUR CUSTOMER EXACTLY WHAT THEY REQUIRE... NOT LESS AND NOT MORE.

It's time to get over yourself and build a customer-center, customer-considerate Customer Sales Machine built *for* your customer, rather selling *to* them.

Unlike the different Customer Marketing Machines and Customer Offer Machines for different industries, Customer Sales Machines are pretty much alike. They will be constructed using the very same components.

AH HA MOMENT ⚡: JUDY

Judy owns a software development company. She was looking at ways to increase her revenue and create a better service for her clients. We knew three things:

1. Judy received most of her clients through referrals

2. Her clients purchased new upgrades every six to 10 years

3. She was a leader in her marketplace because the software had worked flawlessly for many years

Every month Judy stressed about cash flow and revenue. There was no machine in place to create Ideal Prospects. As we coached her, we asked, "What it would happen if you called all your current Ideal Customers and asked them the magic question: 'what other problems or challenges are you experiencing in your systems?' What if they described a problem you're talented to easily solve, and they would purchase that solution because they know you and trust you?"

Sorry to say, Judy never asked the magic question. Instead, she created a service they did not want...which they did not buy. Judy was no better off than before she had spent the time and money to create the unwanted new service. How much happier might Judy be if she'd asked the question and built the business *for her customer* instead of just building a product? How much might her business have grown?

Coaches' Question: Are you selling for or to your Ideal Prospects? If you're selling to them, go back and ask them what their next problem is and if they would consider buying x service from you to solve it. With confirmation, now you create the right customer-centered service.

Sales is not a roll of the dice.

Once your Customer Sales Machine is up, running and humming along, you can hire someone or a team of people to make sales under your supervision. Not until you hear the hum.

YOUR CUSTOMER SALES MACHINE COMPONENTS

Your Customer Sales Machine will likely contain these components:

- Tracking forms
- 30, 60 and 90-day Sales Pipeline
- The Sales Conversation
- The Sales Commitment
- The Follow Up
- Your Sales Mantra

Tracking Forms and Reports—Tracking forms provide a way to follow your Ideal Prospect through your Customer Sales Machine. Tracking demands you document all Ideal Prospect interactions from the first point of entry (call, email, opt-in on your website or landing page, referral, Facebook of LinkedIn follower, etc) through every interaction to ultimately becoming your Ideal Customer or not. When you do, you've tracked the best path to your sale as you're likely to see the same path happen again and again. You've also tracked where your Ideal Prospect stops engaging with you. This is how our Care Managers know only three of 10 inquiries lead to a new Ideal Customer. They track all points of engagement.

A GOOD SALES TRACKING PROCESS HANDS YOU INSIGHTS INTO YOUR BUSINESS YOU NEVER SAW BEFORE.

As you track, you'll discover spots of friction, places where engagement routinely falls away. You'll see what types of email subject lines are opened more frequently and which create little action. You'll know who refers to you, who just walked in the door, who met you at a networking event, who saw you speak, and which advertisements drew their attention.

Your sales tracking form can be as easy as an Excel spreadsheet or as complex as a robust electronic Customer Relationship Management (CRM) system such as Mail Chimp, Constant Contact or Infusionsoft.

A good sales tracking process hands you insights into your business you never saw before and enables you to make changes to test for improvements in your Customer Sales Machine such as:

- More detailed and deeper insights into your Ideal Prospects steps to a sale

- Performance monitors for individual team members and your team as a whole

- More precise revenue projections by understanding potential sales in the pipeline at various stages (30, 60 90 days or more)

- Insights into your Ideal Customer's buying and not buying behavior

- The ability to increase customer satisfaction by addressing their issues and providing customized services to them

Here is an example of how a sales tracking system boosted the revenues of one company.

AH HA MOMENT ⚡: PLASTICS MANUFACTURER

A few years ago, we were working with a $18M plastics manufacturer in California. They invited us to attend their August sales meeting to review their sales system and recommend adjustments. The meeting began promptly at 11:00 am, went through lunch and lasted well into the afternoon. By late afternoon the outcome of the meeting was vague. They had reached no agreements, and yet, the entire management team, both production and sales, were in attendance. A very expensive format, considering people time and actual company downtime.

Most employees in the room did not have the same forms, and many hadn't prepped for the meeting. About half way through the first hour, we asked them how they knew if they had enough sales opportunities in the pipeline to support their targeted 12% growth rate for the current year. The CEO responded, "If we manage to production goals, we will know if we can handle the increase in sales. That way we won't overburden the production line." We then asked them if they were on track for a 12% year over year growth. They answered, "Probably not because we have no idea what sales we will bring in between now and the end of the year."

What??? "Wait a minute. If you have no idea what sales will come in, how can you manage production," we stammered. Basically, they had been managing their entire business by the current production orders. They had no 30, 60 90-day sales pipeline or for that matter any idea of where the next sale would come from. They were running by the seat of their pants.

Over the next six months, we worked with them to implement a sales pipeline with accurate 30, 60 90-day tracking forms which everyone used. We encouraged them to hold separate sales meetings to discuss the pipeline and a separate production meetings to talk about fulfillment. Later that year, the new COO said she couldn't believe how relaxed she felt because she had a sales system which tracked activity and potential customers. Now she could more accurately forecast production which affected the supply chain and the client deliverables.

30-60-90 Day Sales Pipeline—If we asked you how many people are likely to buy from you within 30 days would you have the answer? How about for 60 days? 90 days? Don't know? Without this insight reaching your monthly revenue goal feels like pulling a rabbit out of a hat...every month.

Your business feels arbitrary. You're flying by the seat of your pants. You can't project what's going to happen in your very near future.

Your 30-60-90 day sales pipeline can be as simple as an excel spreadsheet used to track all your conversations with Ideal Prospects with your projection when they will say "yes." If you're talking to your Ideal Prospect who says, "No, not now," and you ask when, they might say something like "Well, after graduation in two weeks. Then I can pay attention to what I need." Two weeks falls within 30 days. You settle on a date and time when you'll call them again three weeks from this call. Put their name, contact information, the nature of your call, next steps and next day to call on your Excel spreadsheet. Put the call on your calendar. When the date comes, call.

If your Ideal Prospect indicates their timeframe to decide looks more like 60 or 90 days out, record the same information and set the date and time for your next call with them.

Now you have your 30-60-90 day sales pipeline.

Of course, people will change their minds. Your 30 day Ideal Prospect, when you call, might tell you graduation caused them to push back other issues they must tackle before solving the problem you're working on with them. They might move back to your 60-day sales pipeline. Then you might call one of your Ideal Prospects who indicated they wouldn't be ready to do anything for 60 days only to discover they are ready to go now. The problem feels too acute not to address now.

Things change. The only way to stay on top of all your opportunities is to track them in your 30-60-90 day sales pipeline.

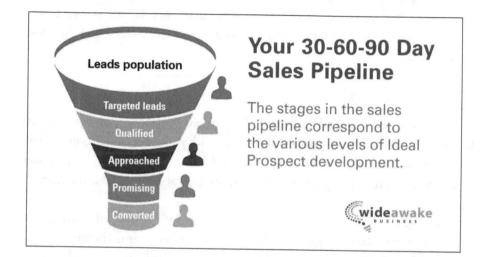

The Sales Conversation—is your verbal dance between you and your Ideal Prospects. Remember you can't sell anything to anyone who does not have a real want coupled with a motivation to buy. People buy what they want, but not always what they need. Our team has worked with thousands of business owners who want to smoothly share their Super Powers and how they solve their Ideal Customer's problem. Through our year of sales training we've noticed two things: (1) once they start to feel comfortable and confident in what they will say, our Ideal Customers say it's way easier to sell than they expected, especially when they know who their customers are, and (2) when they offered products and services with a true and desired impact on their Ideal Customer because the product or service solved a key challenge or problem, their sales increased dramatically.

YOU CAN'T SELL ANYTHING TO SOMEONE WHO DOES NOT HAVE A DESIRE TO BUY.

The Introvert Advantage: What type of person do you think is the most persuasive? An introvert or an extrovert? Well, of course the extrovert! Extroverts have all the words, and they are comfortable in every social situation.

Guess again. In reality, introverts rock in the sales kingdom.

INTROVERTS ROCK IN THE SALES KINGDOM.

Why? Because the introvert knows how to listen. Good sales techniques included listening with third-level listening, listening for what is inferred and not said explicitly. Chris gets asked frequently, "How did you find out so much about the person's life, their marriage, their business, their problems or challenges?" It's simple. We listen...listen for what's being said, and accurately listening for what's not being said. We enter every conversation with curiosity.

Good listening starts with creating powerful questions. Open-ended questions that begin with 'how' or 'what' create an easy way to begin active listening. During many of our speaking engagements we use an interactive role-play exercise to practice the opening of sales conversations. Just the other day at a speaking engagement, Sara, one of the participants, blurted out after the interactive role play "Wow, that was way easier than I expected. I can do that."

Here are a few tips to make your sales conversations go smoothly:

- The phone may feel like it weighs 100 pounds; start your calls with someone you know

- Imagine the phone is light as a feather...it helps

- Be consistent; commit to making calls, put time on the calendar and keep your commitment

- Connect first, sell second

- Use talking points; write them down

The **Sales Commitment**—We call your commitment to yourself to sell your Power Hour, a dedicated hour each week or day, depending on how much time you spend working on your business. Your Power Hour is your non-negotiable appointment with your telephone every day to make sales calls. Think about it. What kind of appointments do you have that are non-negotiable? Tax appointments, car repair, doctors' appointments, jury duty. And why? Because the consequence of not keeping those appointments is extreme. The consequence of not making your sales calls is equally high over the long run. What happens if you, as a business owner, do not make your goals or more importantly you do not make enough revenue to sustain your lifestyle or your business? You might have to get a j-o-b. You might have to lay off your staff. You might not be able to pay yourself which might mean you can't pay your mortgage or child's education. And the list goes on. The consequences should frighten you.

STOP BEING SCARED, INTIMIDATED, RELUCTANT OR INCONSISTENT ABOUT SELLING.

Stop being scared, intimidated, reluctant or inconsistent about selling. Put your Power Hour on your calendar. Write it in stone, whether it's an hour a day or two hours every other day. Whatever works. Make the plan and stick to it.

In your Power Hour, you connect with the Ideal Prospects you've identified. This is time for calling Ideal Prospects, not for researching who you'll call. You call to connect, expand or build relationships, explore the problem they have they want to go away, determine whether the problem is getting better or worse, make appointments and offer insights (but never solutions…that's what you get paid for when they hire you). You call to learn more about them, share thoughts and recommend ways your services will solve their problems. Our experience tells us the Power Hour delivers a 99.9% effective rate for catapulting your business through the roof.

● ● ● ● ● ● ● ● ● ● ● ● ● ● ● ● ● **Sales Sidebar**

We introduce every one of our coaching clients to the Power Hour and monitor its integration into their business. We access their effectiveness and provide accountability if they slip up on their Power Hour commitment. We do this because we **know** it works. It works for us, too. Our Power 100 now lives in our CRM (*Infusionsoft*), and our sales team reviews it every week to map out our strategy for sales calls. Chris has her Power Hour blocked off on her calendar every day, and NOTHING short of an earthquake bumps it off her calendar. We want to show you how to effectively introduce and successfully use the Power Hour in your business, too. This is one of the powerful business-turning work we can do together.

The **Follow Up**—So you have an Ideal Prospect. You have their contact info, perhaps their email address or a phone or cell number. You reach out once to connect. What do you do next? Most business owners do nothing next. No follow up. They actually believe their Ideal Prospect will call them when they are ready to buy. They deceive themselves. Their Ideal Prospect isn't calling even when they say they will. They simply become busy with other things and forget about you.

Hubspot research shows the average sale requires between five and as many as 20 Ideal Prospect interactions before a first purchase occurs. Five to 20!

So what good does it do you to work to get an Ideal Prospect, check in once and then let them go? Why bother to spend your time and money to attract them in the first place? As 80 percent of salespeople give up after one follow-up, lost opportunities turn to found opportunities when you join the 20 percent who actively engage in follow up. Author and motivational speaker Jim Rohn said it best: "The fortune is in the follow-up."

Why are follow-up calls so valuable? Here are four reasons:

- They create and maintain connection with the customer or potential customer

- They build trust and enhance credibility

- They allow for early adjustment to preserve the relationship

- They create another opportunity to serve (and to sell)

If you think of sales as a conversation with your Ideal Customer, then follow-up is a way to keep the conversation going and your Customer Sales Machine in motion.

Your Sales Mantra—There's one last component of your Customer Sales Machine. You'll require a sales mantra, the continuous reminder loop playing in your head as you approach every sales call or conversation. Your sales mantra guides you through the compelling connection between you and your Ideal Customer. Your sales mantra is what you talk about with your Ideal Prospect when you write or speak with them.

A sales mantra consists of five key reminders:

1. Keep it simple; use the words and phrases of your customer, not your professional language…then they can "hear" you

2. Focus on the right activities; not every Ideal Prospect responds to every activity…so pay attention so you can adjust to meet their needs

3. Say it out loud; practice makes permanent…so you feel natural and comfortable as you speak to your Ideal Prospect

4. Track and adjust; when something's not working, figure out why and adjust…so you'll connect better and faster

5. Don't give up; work to have your sales mantra tumble out smoothly as it takes time…you'll feel more and more comfortable and confident the more frequently you groove into your mantra

KEY CONSIDERATIONS TO BUILD YOUR CUSTOMER MACHINE

Your Customer Machine will never be static. Ideal Customers are not static. People change. Markets change. Trends erupt and fade. Tools come and go. Technology advances and perplexes. Competition expands and diminishes.

Therefore, you must always be perceptive to the chaos of today's economy and ever-changing moods of your Ideal Customer. Track and adjust as the changes occur. Don't Give Up!

- Sales Sidebar

Our entire reason for being in Wide Awake Business is to create **easier, simpler and more profitable businesses for our Ideal Customers**. We're really, really, good at it. Because we have GRIT. Angela Duckworth, in her book *GRIT: The Power of Passion and Perseverance*, writes that her research proves talent alone will not ensure success. Passion and perseverance *plus* talent provide the ingredients for true success. Entrepreneurs exemplify GRIT in the truest sense of the word.

We work with talented entrepreneurs and business owners to build their GRIT, in this crazy, chaotic, wonderful world we all choose to work in. That would be you. Yes, this is us selling you again. So, it's not painful, is it? It's informative. We're just continuing to role model for you.

As you build your Customer Machine, let's revisit some of the key points we've discussed. Remember the **guiding principle, the backbone of** *Customertopia:* <u>**Your Customer is the Center of Everything!**</u>

- Where will you find your Ideal Customer?

- What strategies and marketing methods will you use to get your customer's attention?
  - What skills and technology will you need for those methods?
  - How much time and money will be required for each activity?
  - Who will be responsible for executing each strategy?
  - How frequently will you utilize each strategy? On what schedule?

- What offering (s) will you create for your customer?
  - Which offering(s) will address each specific customer need or problem?
  - How do you know this is what the customer needs or wants?
  - Who is responsible for creating each offering?
  - Is there an order or sequence to your offering(s)?
  - How frequently will you offer each product or service?
  - What benefits will the customer receive from each offering?
  - How will you add value to each offering?

- What is included in your Sales System?
  - How will you track and measure sales?
  - How will you use sales data to drive future decisions?

- How will you calculate the return on your time, money and effort for each part of the customer machine?

- Is everyone on the Team clear about their role and responsibility and how it connects to the other components of the machine?

- How do you communicate and make corrections if something in the machine is broken or needs to be changed?

Coaches' Question: Does your business currently have a clear Customer Machine, or are you still doing random activities? Can you describe or diagram that machine? Can everyone on your Team describe it as well? If you don't currently have fully operational Customer Machine, what do you need to do to create one?

Many business owners come to us for coaching when they can no longer sustain or grow their business through random activities they do alone (or with occasional outsourcing). When we sit down with them, in addition to the considerations we list above, we ask them these questions to help them determine how best to design their Customer Machine to suit them and their business.

- *What are you already good at? If you have a team, what are they good at?*

- *What are you already doing consistently? What works?*

- *How are you measuring the performance of your Customer Machine? How can you measure it?*

- *What are your competitors doing that's working? How are they getting customers and what are they offering?*

- *Is your business cyclical? If yes, how do you design around those cycles to keep cash flow consistent?*

- *What do you know you should be doing that you are not doing today?*

- *Is there anything that you are doing that you think you should eliminate?*

The speed at which your Ideal Customer travels through your Customer Machine must match their comfort and pace. How much time does it take the customer to move from lead to prospect to buyer? Do you know? When you have a consistent process, you will track this information to get the answer and then tailor your business process to what your customer requires. At every decision point, a "golden moment" appears, the right time to move the Ideal Customer from one step to the next. Asking for the buying decision too soon or too late results in a loss of trust or credibility, or an abandonment of the process.

AT EVERY DECISION POINT, THERE IS A "GOLDEN MOMENT," THE RIGHT TIME TO MOVE THE CUSTOMER FROM ONE STEP TO THE NEXT.

KNOW YOUR NUMBERS

To really know your Ideal Customer means you also know your numbers. It's simple math. Here's some simple Ideal Customer math: it's a percentage game.

Only a percentage of your leads become Ideal Prospects. Only a certain percentage of your Ideal Prospects will become Ideal Customers. Not every lead will become an Ideal Prospect or Ideal Prospect become an Ideal Customer.

Do you know the percentages for your business? Most business owners don't.

Yet, knowing unveils revelatory knowledge. Knowing increases your efficiency in building your Customer Machine. You see points of friction and eliminate them. You can glean new, useful insights into your Ideal Prospects and Ideal Customers. You know how to gain more Ideal Customers, make more money, reduce your feelings of being overwhelmed, pay yourself more and more frequently, take vacations and feel like a happier person!

Tracking becomes easy when you integrate a system that enables you to track your interactions with leads, Ideal Prospect and your Ideal Customers. One way to do this is with a robust Customer Relations Management (CRM) system. These systems allow you to track your contacts, see which emails they've opened and when, add comments from your sales conversations and list all the services they purchased and when. The most sophisticated systems allow you to enter a variety of details about every individual contact.

Here's an example of what tracking can tell you.

AH HA MOMENT ⚡: SUE

Our client, Sue, a Real Estate Agent, calculated her customer math this way.

Annual Gross Income Goal	$500,000
Average Sales Commission	$12,000
Number of Sales Needed	42
Number of Sales Needed Per Month	4 (allowing for extra)
Percent of Listings Closing Per Month	50%
Active Listings Needed Monthly	8
Percent of Appointments Resulting in Listing	75%
Number of Appointments Needed	11
Percent of Contacts Resulting in Appt	10%
Number of Contacts Needed Monthly	110

What did Sue learn from this math? She discovered to reach her goal she required 12 sales for the year, about four each month. To reach four sales per month she must have eight listings monthly. To get eight listings she had to achieve 11 appointments. And to attain 11 appointments Sue needed to attract 110 possible sellers.

These insights made Sue efficient. She knew precisely what each month must look like to reach her revenue goal. If one month was slow, following months must be more productive. What a great way to work! With full knowledge of what you need to put in motion.

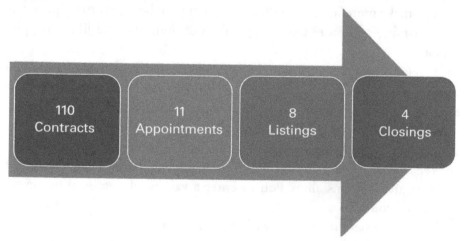

110 Contracts · 11 Appointments · 8 Listings · 4 Closings

Knowing your numbers leads to increased sales through anticipating your customer's needs based on historic trends. Knowing your numbers enables you to successfully lead your Ideal Customer through your Customer Machine.

Your numbers become your forecast. Will things change? You bet. This is a forecast, an estimate. It's not dogma...or Fantasy Island!

Knowing the math feels better, doesn't it? Build your number picture below.

COACHING EXERCISE 24: *Build By The Numbers*

1. List all the activities you typically do for marketing. For each activity, describe what you know about your Ideal Customer that tells you this strategy will be a good match for finding and attracting them.

_____

_____

_____

_____

_____

2. For each activity you listed in #1, list the average number of contacts you achieve using that activity.

_____

_____

_____

_____

_____

3. Now place each activity in #2 above here and indicate how many times you generally do each activity monthly.

_____

_____

_____

_____

4. If there is a required or logical progression between two or more activities, write them in order below. Assign a shape or symbol to each activity.

_____

_____

_____

_____

5. Estimate (or review actual data) the number of contacts from each lead generation activity that result in an expression of interest (opt-in, call, appointment or other). What does this tell you about your Ideal Prospect's pace? Should you make any changes in your process based on this data?

_____

_____

_____

_____

_____

6. Estimate (or review actual data) the number of appointments, calls or other activities that result in a sale.

_____

_____

_____

_____

_____

7. List the average amount of each sale you make. If you prefer, list each product or service you sell separately.

_____

_____

_____

_____

_____

8. Write the amount of gross revenue you want to make in the next 12 months.

Revenue Goal for 2019 _____

Divide that goal by 12 to get the
average monthly revenue you need: _____

9. Calculate the number of sales total or the number of each type you need to meet the monthly revenue goal.

_____

_____

_____

_____

10. Estimate the number of leads you require each month to meet this sales goal (Divide each sale amount by the percentage of leads that convert to sales).

_____

_____

_____

_____

_____

11. Estimate (or review actual data) the number of contacts from each lead generation activity you need to meet the monthly goal for leads.

_____

_____

_____

_____

_____

12.   Complete the chart below with your numbers.

_____	_____	_____	_____
Contracts	Appointments	Listings	Closings

Remember, all these Coaching Exercises are available
to you, along with special offers on our website:
wideawakebusiness.com/resources

CUSTOMER MACHINE SUCCESS STORIES

All through *Customertopia* we have shared Ah Ha Moments to illustrate many points along the way to building your own Customer Machine and enter *Customertopia*. We thought we'd share a capsule version of some of the successes our Ideal Customers achieved once they built their respective Customer Machines. You can see we've worked with a wide variety of businesses, and their Customer Machines differ because they represent different industries. Each business owner designed their Customer Machine to meet the unique needs of their Ideal Customers.

Helen, a Veterinarian—Increased revenue by 50% year over year

We worked with Helen to create and implement customer-focused systems including:

- Regular team building activities to enroll everyone in the vision of growing the practice

- Inviting customers to post reviews on Yelp

- Calling past customers to remind them to set appointments for annual exams and vaccines

- Creating an interactive website with maps, customer reviews, and fresh content

- Reaching agreements with other local vets for managing overflow

- Offering complimentary services and products such as dog washing, kenneling, pet food and vitamins

- Delivering impeccable customer service

William, a CPA—Increased clientele by over 100 clients in one year

William lives with a CPA business that's heavily loaded during tax season and wanted to make sure he engaged his customers throughout the year. His Customer Machine included:

- Building and strengthening team on a regular basis

- Enhancing visibility through SEO, including maps, organic search and back links

- Creating interactive content on his website, including maps, reviews and content

- Actively requesting current customers to refer friends and family

- Offering free training through videos and webinars for customers

- Offering complementary services such as bookkeeping and creating new business entities

- Providing timely follow up and decreasing response lag time

Bernie, an Audiologist—Increased revenue by 65% during his slowest month of the year

Bernie's cash flow was uneven. He wanted to create more opportunities for revenue during his slowest months. Bernie's Customer Machine included these elements:

- Scheduling regular follow-ups with past customers to encourage purchase of replacements, upgrades or new batteries

- Creating an active referral system with physicians

- Introducing a structured referral system with past clients via a letter campaign, in person visits and calls

- Designing and integrating an impeccable customer service plan for both sales and clinical teams

- Leading a systematic calling program to set appointments with past clients

- Requesting customers to post reviews on Yelp

- Stepping up to an active social media presence, including Facebook

- Increasing visibility through sponsorship of local charitable events

- Hosting local classes and workshops

NEXT STOP, CUSTOMERTOPIA

Can you feel the momentum building? Once you mastered the *Customertopia* Mindset, learned to **Think Like Your Customer, Act Like Your Customer and Build For Your Customer**, your business will transform. You'll enter *Customertopia*.

Building for your customer means **every process and every strategy center on what best serves your ideal customer**. You make it easy for them to find you, be attracted to you, recognize you have what they want (and what they need) and take the right actions to solve their problem.

YOUR BUSINESS IS BECOMING EASIER, SIMPLER AND MORE PROFITABLE EVERY DAY.

You've created a clear and consistent path, a Customer Machine, your Ideal Customer can follow from initial contact to a long-term relationship where you consistently find new and better ways to serve them. Best of all, you don't have to do it alone anymore because your Customer Machine is organized, documented and easy to follow. You can make changes easily and confidently because you have a process for measuring success and getting customer feedback.

PART FIVE

An Easier, Simpler, More Profitable Business

At the end of the day…a long, hard, dog-tired day…what each of us want as small business owners is an easier, simpler, more profitable business. That's *Customertopia*.

You have customers, and they are the right kind of customers. They come more easily because you're thinking, acting and building with them in the center of everything you do. Complex systems and steps are eliminated as the path to customers becomes simpler to see, jettisoning the unnecessary. And certainly, more customers arriving more easily and simply will absolutely lead you straight to a more profitable business.

As we write this, we've just returned from our three-day leadership retreat, Lead Her Up Retreat, for successful small business women. Many have created their success on the backs of their own labor. Yes, some have teams. Yes, they have systems. Yes, they are profitable. What struck us was how ready they were for the next maturation of their businesses—to create easier and simpler businesses where they design and deliver more impactful aspirations and pain elimination for their Ideal Customers, where they elevate their leadership of self, team and legacy. All of which becomes possible because they are more profitable.

We have a financial expression we use within Wide Awake Business. We talk about ROM and ROC—Return on Martha and Return on Chris. What are we earning individually and as a company for the hours we put in? As the leader of your business, there's a return on you, too.

What does your ROY—Return on You—look like? For the hours of work you're putting in, for the waking moments in the middle of the night as you press to solve a dilemma, for the vacations you've surrendered or sacrificed to get something out the door or tend to a problem "only you can solve", what does your ROY look like?

For most small business owners, it's dismal. You're overworked, overwhelmed with too many roads leading to you. Customers aren't as plentiful as you'd like (hopefully, you're not one of those folks who say "if only they'd just show up...because you know that's not how it works). You don't feel you can afford more team member because where would the money come from? And you might not be paying yourself (or paying yourself enough) so how could you pay others?

Can we share some truth about hiring team and paying when you don't have the money? Please sit down because what we're going to say sounds odd, or impossible, or just straight-up crazy.

Every successful business we've worked with (and there are over 5,324 of them as we write this) has actually *grown* when they've committed funds to hiring new team. Even when they didn't know how they could possibly pay for the team. When they couldn't see where the money would come from. When they felt their challenged financially.

They grew.

How???

It happens because the new team member takes over some task the owner shouldn't be doing, enabling the owner to deliver higher value work to the business. More sales happen. More money comes in.

What is higher value work?

You deliver greater value to your work when you substantially reduce the time you spend moving papers around, doing administrative work, doodling on new programs you could create though you're not selling the ones you have, checking out the frig to see if any new foods have miraculously appeared since the last time you looked, keeping a piece of work for yourself to do because you can "do it faster than anyone else in the office," and you-know-what-you're-doing-you-shouldn't-be-doing.

Sure, many pieces of paper require you, as the owner, to touch. Yet, most of your admin time delivers little value to your business. Doodling new programs is interesting, but is it time better spent than selling your current Ideal Prospects? And, trust us, there's nothing new in the frig. And, sure, you might be able to do it faster than anyone else in the office, but if you keep doing this work, you'll always be doing it as you haven't taken the time to train someone. You're torpedoing your ROY.

With this kind of "stuff" off your plate you can move to the higher value work of building your Customer Machine, including speaking at conferences or events, building a strong affiliate network of people who refer to you, creating a Facebook or LinkedIn marketing strategy that engages your Ideal Customer and setting the strategy, tone, values, and culture of the business. You'll spend more time selling and turning your Ideal Prospects into Ideal Customers.

Leading in your business.

This higher value work, when you engage, brings in more customers and more customers mean more money and more money pays for the new team you brought in.

Yes, you'll be doing the leap of faith thing. The new team member will arrive before the money has arrived. So, you've got to have your plan in place to bring in the new team member and get you out to deliver the higher value, revenue-producing work that pays for them (and might pay you more, too).

Following the step-by-step process that forms Customertopia will enable you to create an easier, simper and more profitable business. That enables you to hire more team and bring in efficient systems to build a Customer Machine which makes your business simpler. You can step up to higher value work, making your business more profitable.

In the end you have what you want. Fewer roads leading to you. Fewer two a.m. jolts of worry about where the money will come from. A plate that's not overflowing with lower value work that others could be doing, freeing you for work more suited to the CEO/President.

YOU DON'T HAVE TO DO THIS ALL BY YOURSELF

Customertopia will enable many small business owners to read, absorb and go out and do. Other owners will read and ask, "can't someone just do this for me?"

Yes, we can work with you in a variety of ways to turn your business into Customertopia. We can work with you to:

- Unmask your very best Ideal Customer

- Determine their Buying Motivators, their pain point or desire for a particular goodness (pleasure)

- Unearth their Aspirations and Problems

- Adjust your marketing and sales conversations to focus on what they want versus what you know they need including:
  - Brochure copywriting
  - Website development and copy creation
  - LinkedIn strategies

- Build your Customer Machine including:
  - Aligning your steps to a Sales System
  - Identify the best sales path to your Ideal Customer
  - Improve your hiring and team building system

We have a team of expert Mentors, Coaches, branding and positioning specialists, copywriters, designers, website developers, CPAs, incorporation experts, virtual CFOs, book publishers, team-building experts and more waiting to serve you to create an easier, simpler, more profitable you.

EXPLORE WHAT'S POSSIBLE FOR YOU

If Customertopia has opened your eyes yet you really want the experts to tackle much of this for you (higher ROY), your next step is simple. Accept our sincere invitation to have an exploratory conversation about your business and its next steps to profitability.

A 30-minute strategy call will give you one-on-one time with Wide Awake Business experts to identify your best steps to create the ROY you desire. During the exploratory call…no obligations tangling…your business development strategist will rapidly determine where you are versus what you want to be, plus identify at least one adjustment to get you moving faster to the business you want.

You can grab our invitation for your exploratory strategy session in one of several ways:

- Call our office at 530-613-5342

- Drop us an email at Chris@wideawakebusiness.com

- Drop this URL into your browser and set up your exploratory strategy session on-line: www.meetme.so/ChrisWideAwake

Candidly, most books don't call for action. This one demands it. You're completing all the Coaching Exercises and putting what you're learning into practice. Or you've read everything, want everything and just crave some expert to step in and deliver much of this for you as it's not your area of expertise. You're a great accountant, yoga instructor, care manager, real estate agent, ghost writer, wine tour operator, book publisher, or whatever you're an expert in.

That's fine.

You don't have to do this all by yourself.

If you are one of those individuals—and we do hope you are—who is willing to stop, turn in a new direction and start attracting customers the way they want to be attracted, then we were meant to work together.

We know it's difficult to see your business as others see it. We bring "fresh eyes". It's tough to break old habits or the way you were trained. We bring "new ways." And frankly, customers change all the time—they are people after all, and we people are changing daily. That makes it tricky to find the "new new" thing that's not the latest flashy trend and has staying power. We bring the "staying power."

INVESTMENT OR EXPENSE

The next choice is yours. Was this book a business expense—a nice read—or is it an investment because you put these steps into action to create your own Customertopia?

This book was intended to be more than just ink on paper. Our goal is to open your eyes to what your customers really want and how you can give them precisely what they really want to create an easier, simpler and more profitable business for you.

If your eyes are open, your mind is curious, and your imagination stimulated, commit to follow through.

We're going to tell you right now only action will deliver your Customertopia. Reading is nice. Doing something is superior and takes you really where you want to go, doesn't it? One step, then another, then the next. Pretty soon you're in big-time motion.

Read the book again, and this time do the exercises, write your notes and put pen to paper to make this information your knowledge. And reach out to us to take your results above and beyond, to take you fully into an easier, simpler, more profitable business by building your own Customertopia.

We couldn't be more excited for your success.

EPILOGUE

We've shared everything we know and work on with our own customers in the belief this knowledge will hand you the path to where you want your business to be. The key...the central theme throughout Customertopia...is your customer must be the centerpiece of your business, of everything you do and say. Most importantly, the centerpiece of your heart and, therefore, your aligned actions. Walk the talk, my friends.

Do we occasionally stumble from the Customertopia path? Absolutely. When we do, we pick ourselves up, brush off our dust and try again in a better, more customer-centered way. You'll stumble, too, and hopefully, dust yourself off and improve. We are alike in that way, you and us.

What's contained in this book is what we wish people had told us (if they even knew) when we were getting our MBA, working for big companies and out working on our own. Sigh. People didn't tell us. We suspect because they didn't know. Now you do. Go put it to good use.

And so it is.

Go forth and do great things,

Martha Hanlon
Chris Williams

ADDITIONAL CUSTOMER MACHINES

THE DIRECT SALES CUSTOMER MACHINE

Have you ever participated in companies like Mary Kay, Arbonne International, Avon, BeachBody, Cabi, Send Out Cards, Isagenix, Nikken, NuSkin, Pampered Chef or Traveling Vineyard? If you have, you belonged to a direct sales company. Thousands of direct sales companies exist, offering everything from wellness products to wine to lotions to you name it.

As a distributor for a direct sales company, your business sells products the company creates, and you use their systems to order, buy and replenish products. You're not an employee of the direct sales company; you're an independent distributor tied to them through a contract. Your job is selling the products face-to-face away from any retail store location. If you've never been a direct sales company distributor, perhaps you've attended an in-home shopping party or presentation.

If you recognize your business in this description, you might not think you require a Customer Machine identified by us because the direct sales company leads you to believe they have everything you require to market and sell their products (which is how you make money). They offer brochures, banners, sample products, sales instructions and more. Yet, every direct sales business distributor we've worked with discovers at some point they must create their own Customer Machine, even if it's augmented by materials from the company.

So here it is. The Customer Machine for Direct Sales people:

- Decode your company compensation plan

- Seek out a company mentor above you in your distribution family, someone you want to be in six months; ask for their support and show them your drive to advance
  - ○ Do EXACTLY what your mentor tells you to do; mirror their success plan

- Create a list of 100 people you know, could refer to you or could affiliate with you because they have your Ideal Customer
  - ○ Begin a systematic outreach to all of them
  - ○ Allocate time every day, every week to reaching out
  - ○ Follow up; people will probably not buy the first time you speak with them
  - ○ Follow up again and again; people will likely not become one of your distributors the first several times you approach them with the idea

THE COME-TO-YOUR-HOME SERVICES
CUSTOMER MARKETING MACHINE

Plumbers, HVAC technicians, electricians, pest control, washer repair, masons and gardeners, we're talking about you. We've all called them all to our home at one point of another. If you have an I-come-to-your-home business, we're talking about your Customer Machine right now.

- Social proof

- SEO for organic search, coupled with back links and retargeting ads

- Active community involvement

- Advertising magnetics or stickers to leave on the appliance

- Automatic yearly inspection plans

- Networking

AH HA MOMENT ⚡: EVENT PARTICIPANT

At a speaking event, we were talking about advertising tools, specifically direct mail. A pest control owner raised his hand and said he did not believe in direct mail. He had been using the same direct mail piece for years and never got one client.

We questioned him and said if the direct mail piece did not yield clients, "what do you suppose could be wrong? The copy? The frequency? The Ideal Customer profile? Or direct mail content?"

He had been using the same direct mail piece for seven years, and it never yielded new customers. He had been doing the wrong activity for years.

We're not sure the gentleman had an Ah Ha moment, or if he's still using the same old, ineffective direct mail piece. We just had an Ah Ha moment...if it ain't working, move to something proven!

THE ON-LINE BUSINESS CUSTOMER MACHINE USING AMAZON, EBAY, ETSY AND THE LIKE

Do you sell using Amazon, eBay, Etsy or Pinterest to name a few?
Try on this Customer Machine:

- Design and build a clean, easy-to-explore website; consider colors, fonts and presentation of products

- Remove friction from your sales; it's all about the customer experience

- Use key words and SEO to drive visitors to your site

- Search for a mentor to show you the ropes, someone who's accomplished what you want to accomplish

- Sell products and services you believe in

- Use customer-centered copy on your site; never forget your Ideal Customer's favorite topic is them

THE ON-LINE BUSINESS CUSTOMER MACHINE

Is your primary way to attract new Ideal Prospects on-line advertising on Facebook or other sites?

On-line businesses seem so desirable to many business owners. You don't have to speak with anyone, pick up the phone and call, book speaking engagements or leave your home to network. You could stay in your jammies all day long.

All of that is true. However, relying exclusively or primarily on an online business model demands a bold, technology-savvy person or someone with the budget for a tech team. If that's not you, find a team or another path to come-to-market.

If you're still "all in" on an online business model, here's your Customer Machine:

- Create a super-specific profile of your Ideal Customer on the platform of your choice; put in characteristics of your Ideal Customer with a goal of about one million people fitting that profile

- Test as many as six different ads to attract Ideal Prospects; then analyze which worked best and which showed anemic results; eliminate the poor one and create a replacement

- Before you make any offer, determine what your end goal is; what do you want to sell ultimately online; then build your offers backwards from your end goal

- Make a highly, highly compelling free offer through your ad; use photos or pictures and very few words to make your offer

- Make an offer for a product with a very low price point; remember they don't know you at all and this is like dating

- If they don't take your offer, make it again; you never know

- If they still don't take your offer, make a different offer

- If they buy, celebrate, deliver a superior product with amazing customer support and service

- If they don't buy, keep them in your "warm" communication cycle

---

Remember, all these Coaching Exercises are available to you, along with special offers on our website: wideawakebusiness.com/resources

ACKNOWLEDGMENTS

Like most labors of love, this book would not exist without the effort and support of many people. Everyone on this page has touched us and this book in some meaningful way. We could not be more grateful.

Gail Dixon, you are a brave, courageous woman to take on the task of understanding and interpreting the Wide Awake Business mind. Such a talent and daring are rare in any individual. You make us smarter and more intuitive.

Cheryl Lentz, you waded through every word, every comma, every everything in this book to find the ways to make it easier to read, understandable to this book owner, and applicable to everyone who wants an easier, simpler, more profitable business using the principles of Customertopia.

To Kathy Henry, Tim Petree, Paul Meinardus, Marnie Giorgi, Kelly Toole, Debra Jason, Andrea Feinberg, Wendy Watkins and Ruth Mannschreck you make us wiser, bolder and more heart-centered. Keep being brave and bold, doing customer-centered work and making Martha and Chris look pretty darned good.

To our families for understanding when the lights were still on in the office when the lights were out in the rest of the house.

To friends who said, "Do it!" and supported us through the process. YaYas...you know.

And to Jasper and Tally for not always barking when Martha's on the phone with a customer.

RESOURCES

We could put all the worksheets right here in the book for you to tear out, but who wants to work on 6" x 9" pieces of papers! So we've placed everything on our website available to all of our readers. You can pick up all the worksheets and resources in this book for free at https://wideawake business.com/resources.

And remember our complimentary invitation to you. Call for a 30-minute business review. IIt's our invitation to you to receive everything you want from your business. It's why we're here.

You have several ways you can connect with us. What's your preference?

- Book directly with Chris using her appointment calendar link: www. meetme.so/ChrisWideAwake

- Drop us an email at: Chris@wideawakebusiness.com

- Call our office: 530-613-5342

ABOUT THE AUTHORS

 **Martha Hanlon** sees and hears what most businesses struggle to uncover what truly motivates a customer to buy...or not. She's a thought-provoking business development and marketing expert who spots trends and breaks a lot of business "rules" to deliver fresh results. Her forward-thinking has led to the identification of nine business development leverages that create an easier, simpler and *more profitable* business...the fastest path to customers. Fun, engaging and a bit irreverent, Martha is passionate about supporting small businesses by teaching them how to engage customers, market and do it as much as *$4^1/_2$ x faster* than what they are doing now.

Martha has founded three marketing companies, after years leading product management and marketing divisions in Corporate America. She's worked with more than 4,891 companies from Fortune 100 to VC-backed start-ups to the auto dealer down the street to build brands, create new services and generate customers. She's mentored hundreds of small business owners, guiding them to a smarter path for customers and wealth.

Martha has an MBA from The Wharton School, University of Pennsylvania and a B.S. from Duquesne University. She is a sought-after writer, international speaker, facilitator and trainer. She is the primary author of *money-Making Marketing,* the #1 Amazon Best Seller, *Customertopia: How to Create and Easier, Simpler, More Profitable Business,* and the #3 Amazon Marketing Best Seller, *Customers Are the Answer to Everything.* She currently sits on several Boards.

Oh...and ask her about the Thin Mint Plan.

Chris Williams is an expert in generating customers and boosting revenue for small to medium-sized businesses.

As a sought-after international speaker, business consultant and best-selling author, along with Martha Hanlon of Customers Are the Answer to Everything, Chris applies the sales systems and strategies she developed in here corporate career to support business owners in a wide range of industries around the globe, resulting in more customers and higher revenues. Since 2008 nearly 5,000 business owners have relied on the expertise of Chris and Wide Awake Business to boost their revenues by more than $538 million dollars.

Small business owners connect with Chris as she's shown so many owners their path to success, plus she's "walked in their shoes," creating three successful businesses of her own. They receive a "system" to transform their bottom line. Chris' style connects and encourages action, making businesses easier, simpler and more profitable.

Made in USA - Kendallville, IN
1044499_9781732938236